CONTENTS

THE IMPLICATIONS OF THE EVOLUTION OF EUROPEAN INTEGRATION FOR UK LABOUR MARKETS

by

Michael Gold
and Duncan Matthews

National Institute of Economic and Social Research

The views expressed in the report are the authors' and do not
necessarily reflect those of the Department.

Preface

This document is the final report on a three-year research project undertaken by the National Institute of Economic and Social Research for the Department of Employment. The objective of this research was:

'to improve understanding of the implications of the European Community policy and emerging regulation relating to the labour market and the programme by which it is determined in order to assist policy makers in helping to shape policy in Europe and adjust to it in the UK'

The programme of work had three main aims to help achieve this objective:

1. 'to ensure that the [Employment] Department is abreast of the current development of EC single-market proposals, including the social field, and to contribute analysis of their likely impact on the UK, particularly in the labour market';

2. 'to provide an insight into the way EC policy is formulated and how policy formulation can be influenced'; and

3. 'to ensure that best use is made of the wider ESRC initiative into the evolution of rules for a single market for addressing the interests of the UK, particularly in the social field'.

These aims have been fulfilled in two ways. The first has been addressed through a series of reports and case studies during the research programme, most of which have been presented in seminars at the Employment Department and widely discussed. These are listed in Appendix II.

Linkage with the ESRC research programme has been achieved through the participation of Employment Department officials in the research network and its meetings, direct contact with various of the researchers and the dissemination of the research results.

The present document draws together the various reports and case studies. The report has four main sections. The first sets out the origins of the differences in approach to social and labour policy and the differences in structures to implement it between the UK and its continental partners. It emphasises that there is no single continental approach but that there are some far-reaching common threads from traditions of Social and Christian Democracy, for example. In particular it explains how the social dimension in Continental Europe has come to be dominated by the problems of employees rather than by the wider concerns of the disadvantaged, whether employed, unemployed or outside the labour force as is the case in the UK.

The next three sections turn to social policy within the European Union itself. They begin in section 2 with an exploration of how policy has actually been developed in practice, looking at the role of the various institutional actors including the Commission, the Council of Ministers and the national governments. Two of the features which it focuses on are the role of experts called in to produce the initial draft of the legislation and the role of lobbyists, whether firms, European organisations or other sectional groups. There is a clear lesson in this experience. Good ideas alone are insufficient for them to be adopted as policy. They have to be presented and applied at the right time in the places where the decisions are taken. It is clear that involvement at an early stage is important. Once the Commission publishes its initial policy document it is already much more difficult to have an impact.

At the final decision-making end of the policy spectrum lies the Presidency of the Council. In section 3 we analyse the constraints on the formulation of policy through the Council. Adopting a case study approach to the work of the 1986 Presidency, we investigate the Commission's responses to the Council Resolution on an Action Programme on employment growth.

In understanding the impact of social and labour policy it is essential to look beyond the topics of agreement to the extent of change in behaviour that they imply in practice. In section 4 we show that even those measures which have been agreed are not necessarily having the effect anticipated, not just because of the well-known slowness of some member states to transpose EC legislation into domestic law but because that legislation is ineffective, either because it is not enforced or because the form of transposition is such that compliance with the letter of the law can still enable firms in some countries to avoid making the intended changes.

However, the work programme for this project has involved far more than just the research on the various topics laid out in the report. The researchers have been involved in the development of policy during the three years of the programme, initially, for example, through an analysis of the lessons to be learned from the experience of the 1986 Presidency of Council so that the Department could be better prepared for what it could (and could not) achieve during the UK Presidency in the second half of 1992.

The researchers have also provided the Employment Department with working papers on developments in the EC such as the discussions on the White Paper on Growth, Competitiveness and Employment (NIESR, 1993) and as background for the preparations for the 1992 UK Presidency (Matthews, 1992).

In recent years there has been a period of some reassessment by EU member states of the scale and speed at which they wish new initiatives to be introduced. Different positions and viewpoints are, for example, reflected in the Delors White Paper on Growth, Competitiveness and Employment (Commission of the EC, 1994a), the OECD Jobs Study (OECD, 1994a) and the paper by the United Kingdom on Growth, Competitiveness and Employment in the European Community (Employment Department/HM Treasury, 1993). This report acknowledges these differing views and positions.

Numerous acknowledgements are due in a Report of this kind: they include Ingo Albrecht and Soterios Soteri (NIESR), the European Foundation for the Improvement of Living and Working Conditions (that financed concurrent research on participation in European multinational companies), David Mayes, who devised the original research project on which this report is based, the various members of the Department of Employment Steering Group and the following members of the International Advisory Panel to the project which met on 6th March 1992 and 6th May 1993:

Andrew Britton (then Director of the National Institute of Economic and Social Research); Arnout de Koster (Vormingscentrum ANPKB, Brussels); Erik de Gier (TNO, Leiden); Mark Hall (Industrial Relations Research Unit, University of Warwick); Philippe Meyer (Consultant Europe Sociale et Ressources Humaines, Ville d'Avray); John Morley (Directorate-General V, Commission of the European Communities, Brussels).

The views expressed in this Report are the authors' own and do not necessarily reflect any that may be held by the National Institute, the Department of Employment or the individual members of the International Advisory Panel. The research was completed in December 1994 and reflects the state of play at that time.

Section 1
Overview of EC Social and Labour Policy

The Community Charter of Fundamental Social Rights (Commission of the EC, 1992b) - adopted by 11 of the 12 EC member states at the Strasbourg summit in December 1989 as a 'Solemn Declaration' - focussed attention on the social dimension of the EC in a way which had been unprecedented until then.

The institutions of the EC had never before attempted to draw up anything like the Social Charter even though other international bodies such as the International Labour Organisation and the Council of Europe have long and respected traditions in attempting to establish general principles of employment rights. Whilst the first social action programme of Directorate-General V of the European Commission (responsible for employment, industrial relations and social affairs) dates back to 1974, debates on social and labour policy until then had tended to centre on specific initiatives, notably equal treatment, industrial participation and health and safety.

The Social Charter, however, was intended to lay a foundation for the European social dimension by establishing a set of rights systematically applicable to all workers and to certain groups of marginalised people across all member states: its accompanying social action programme proposed 47 individual measures grouped under thirteen separate headings, such as the labour market, employment and remuneration, social protection and vocational training, as well as under more familiar headings like equal treatment and health and safety. It also covered action for children and adolescents, the elderly and the disabled (Commission of the EC, 1989).

In addition to these substantive areas, the Social Charter helped focus attention on certain procedural issues as well. Its supporters maintained that its chances of implementation were severely limited if unanimous voting on the Council of Ministers were required to adopt the majority of its proposals. Therefore, it was argued, majority voting should be extended to cover all social policy initiatives, not just health and safety as was then the case. Without majority voting, any one member state could veto proposals which were otherwise supported by all the rest.

The Social Charter therefore sparked off a double controversy: debate raged both round the substantive issues - the merits and demerits of individual measures - as well as round the procedural issues and the alleged 'democratic deficit' within the EC institutions which might hinder their implementation.

This chapter has the following objectives in providing an overview of EC social and labour policy: to examine the social policy provisions contained in the EEC Treaty; to outline the stages through which EC social policy has evolved; to clarify the areas of social policy contained in the Social Charter; and to examine the possible impact of the Maastricht summit on EC social policy.

Social Provisions in the EEC Treaty

It is as well to recall that the objectives of the European Communities (EC), as laid down in Article 2 of the EEC Treaty, are primarily economic - they are defined as 'a harmonious and balanced development of economic activities, sustainable and non-inflationary growth reflecting the environment, a high degree of convergence of economic performance, a high level of employment and social protection, the raising of the standard of living and the quality of life, the economic and social cohesion and solidarity among member states'.

The main provisions concerning social policy in the Treaty can, in consequence, be viewed at least partly as serving these ends.

They govern: free movement of workers (Articles 48-51); right of establishment (particularly in relation to the self-employed) (Articles 52-58); freedom to provide services (Articles 59-66); social provisions (Articles 117-122); European Social Fund (Articles 123-128); and economic and social cohesion (Articles 130A-130E).

The principle governing the social provisions of the EEC Treaty - our main focus here - is encapsulated in Article 117, which is worth quoting in full:

'Member states agree upon the need to promote improved working conditions and an improved standard of living for workers, so as to make possible their harmonisation while the improvement is being maintained.

'They believe that such a development will ensue not only from the functioning of the common market, which will favour the

harmonisation of social systems, but also from the procedures provided for in this Treaty and from the approximation of provisions laid down by law, regulation or administrative action.'

The ambiguity of the second paragraph is noteworthy. On the one hand, 'the functioning of the common market' will help to improve working conditions and standards, but, on the other, 'law, regulation or administrative action' is also required to attain the desired end. Broadly, the former, neo-liberal stance has been invoked over the years by certain member states, employers' organisations and other interests wishing to curb the activities of the Commission in social policy, whilst the Commission, supported principally by the labour movement across the member states, has justified its varied activities in the social field by reference to the latter, more interventionist approach. Clashes over the interpretation of this paragraph have therefore been numerous.

However, it can also be argued that these ambiguities do not only create but also reflect certain tensions at the heart of EC policy formulation, not least the jealousy of member states to keep power over key areas in their own hands. Indeed, an examination of the stages through which EC social policy has evolved - see below - reveals a Commission intent on gradually widening its competence, but member states - often acting through the Council of Ministers - equally intent on preventing it.

Meanwhile, the European Court of Justice has played its own part in interpreting EC-level social legislation over the years through a growing body of case law, whilst employers and organised labour have participated in these developments both informally and through their representation on the Economic and Social Committee. Broadly, labour - which is well organised at EC level - has supported the Commission in its attempts to create the social dimension through legislation, whilst the employers, a more inchoate grouping, have expressed strong reservations over this approach, preferring voluntary methods instead.

Generally, we can identify at least three sources of tension in relation to social policy:

Supranational and national interests

The first, which we have already mentioned, lies in the tension between supranational bodies like the various parts of the Commission, the European Parliament and the European Court of Justice which take an EC-level overview on the one hand, and intergovernmental bodies, like the Council, which represent the national interests of member states on the other. The reality is, of course, far more complex than this since member states will frequently disagree amongst themselves on the Council over particular issues. Some of the member states, more in line with the Directorate-General V's social philosophy than others, will form more or less permanent alliances with that part of the Commission, lodging objections to detail only in specific circumstances, whilst others, more concerned with issues of sovereignty and erosion of powers, adopt a critical stance in principle in relation to Commission proposals.

Social philosophies

Secondly, we can identify wide variations in the social philosophies, traditions and legal practices of the different member states. We can make a broad distinction, following Teague (1989, pp. 66), between the 'social protectionist aims' (of the DG V) and the 'deregulatory outlook of the British Government' in the 1980s, but we can go further too in several ways.

– The social protectionist perspective itself covers Socialist, Social Democratic and Christian Democratic philosophies, all of which broadly accept the principle of intervention, whilst disagreeing, of course, over the degree necessary or desirable. So, for example, in the European Parliament, the Christian Democrats (operating under the banner of the European People's Party) frequently support the Commission's proposals in the social field and vote alongside the Socialist Group. Notions of industry as a collaborative enterprise between employers and employees and the need for a statutory basis for workers' rights are widely shared across the left/centre-right spectrum, even though policies on economic policy may differ sharply. This perspective can be contrasted with the non-interventionist market based approach of the Conservative Government in the UK which has objected to both the setting down of basic rights (such as in the Social Charter) and to their content.

– In addition, we can identify different traditions of legal regulation. Following Due et al (1991) we can distinguish three principal systems across the member states:

• The *Roman-German* system in which the state plays a central role in industrial relations and the constitution guarantees 'a core of fundamental rights and freedoms, constituting the foundation of national industrial relations' (Due et al, 1991, pp. 90). Comprehensive labour market legislation governs areas like working time, employee representation and so on (examples include

Belgium, France, Germany, Italy and the Netherlands).

- The *Anglo-Irish* system in which the role of the state is limited and, although there are comprehensive rights against discrimination on the basis of sex and race and comprehensive health and safety laws, abstention from regulation of labour markets is the tradition. Minimum pay is dealt with through a system of income support that covers the whole population whether or not in the labour market. It is acknowledged that 'traditional features of the Irish system owe much to its origins in the United Kingdom' (von Prondzynski, 1992, p. 70).

- The *Nordic* system in which the state again plays a limited role in industrial relations, but the 'basic agreement' - concluded by employers and unions - instead provides the foundation. The state intervenes in labour market regulation only when requested by the employers and unions (the only member state of the EC currently in line with this model is Denmark, though Finland, Norway and Sweden also conform).

Clearly, the UK, Ireland and Denmark stand apart from their EC partners when compared in this way - as indeed they do in relation to the Commission which tends to reflect the thinking behind the predominant Roman-German model.

The existence of such varying industrial relations systems within a European setting is widely accepted, even though their boundaries may fluctuate and the terminology may vary. For example, Ferner and Hyman (1992b) recognise that these systems have in recent years come under serious pressures, some convergent some divergent. The effects of intensifying international competition have not, for example, been straightforwardly uniform on national systems owing to varying patterns of state ownership, sectoral distribution of economic activity and so on. To be taken into account also are the influence of the political sphere, long-term historical developments and 'institutional persistence', especially when enshrined in the legal system (Streeck, 1987). Nevertheless, Ferner and Hyman identify three different 'systems' from amongst all these ambiguities: there are systems that are strong and inflexible (such as the UK); strong and flexible (Germany, the Netherlands and Scandinavia); and those that are relatively weak from the point of view of institutional regulation (Italy and France). Both Due et al and Ferner and Hyman accept the distinctiveness of the Anglo-Irish system, even though they disagree over the boundaries of the rest.

Within each member state, different political parties, on forming governments, will naturally interpret these traditions and systems differently. The Conservative Government in the UK, for example, which took office in 1979 reflected a non-interventionist market based approach in marked contrast to the Socialist/Social Democratic approach of the Labour Government which it defeated even though, of course, they were both operating in the same Anglo-Irish tradition.

Employers and unions
Thirdly, we can refer to the clash of interests between employers' organisations and unions. There is a certain affinity of interest between the DG V of the Commission and the unions not shared by the employers (reasons for which we explore below) which, coupled with the unions' superior organisation at EC-level, has led to tensions between the social partners. In recent years this has centred on the form and content of the Social Charter and the comparative merits of legislation and collective agreements in regulating labour markets.

To these we could add other tensions, such as those centring on criticisms that EC social policy focuses too heavily on the rights of employed people in relation to the rights of the unwaged (such as the unemployed and pensioners). But enough has been said to establish the main point here, namely that whilst the ambiguity of the Treaty has certainly helped to fuel controversies regarding the direction of EC social policy over the last three or four decades, it also reflected the original concern of the member states to contain the power of the Commission.

Stages of EC Social and Labour Policy

Broadly speaking, the development of EC social policy since 1958 - the year the EEC Treaty took effect - falls into four stages: 1958-72; 1972-80; 1980-87; and post-1987[1].

Stage 1: 1958-1972

The first stage has been characterised as one of 'benign neglect' (Mosley, 1990), a period during which harmonisation of social policy was left to the functioning of the common market itself, against a background of relatively low unemployment and sustained economic growth.

However, this view is rather misleading, since it tends to obscure the reasons underlying the neglect, if such it was. Indeed, in certain areas - particularly those linked to the economic objectives of the Treaty for which a legal base had been given - DG V of the Commission was able to act in relation to 'vocational training, the free movement of labour and the application of the social security measures to those most immediately concerned and equal pay' (Collins, 1975, p. 186). Measures were also adopted to set up the European Social Fund.

Steps were also taken to improve the field of health and safety. In 1959, under the terms of the Treaty establishing the European Atomic Energy Community, a Directive was adopted protecting the public and workers from ionising radiations and, three years later, in 1962, an Industrial Health and Safety Division was set up within DG V, the Directorate-General within the Commission responsible for employment, industrial relations and social affairs. Subsequently the first Directive on the classification, packaging and labelling of dangerous substances was adopted in 1967, as well as Recommendations covering the protection of young people at work and facilities for industrial medicine, amongst other areas.

However, it was not long before the Commission was clashing with the member states represented on the Council. For example, in the Council debate in April 1964, the Commission was warned against extending its powers under Article 118 - it was told that social security fell within the remit of national governments alone and that it therefore had no competence in this field and, furthermore, it could not submit Recommendations on the subjects covered in the Article. At this point relationships between the Commission and the Council broke down, and the Social and Labour Affairs Council did not meet again until December 1966, over two and a half years later, despite the efforts of the European Parliament which had already registered its frustration at the lack of advances being made.

This crisis was, however, merely a sideshow in comparison with the French boycott of the Council between July 1965 and January 1966, a protest at what the French perceived as infringements of their national interests and an expansion generally of the DG V's competence. Once this was eventually resolved, a compromise on social policy was reached in December 1966 by the Council and a humbled Commission, the most important aspect of which was that the Council was to determine the studies to be undertaken by the Commission.

From 1966 onwards, there was a shift in the Commission's emphasis away from the 'social' towards the 'economic' - that is, away from an attempt to secure social policy as an end in itself towards greater consideration of its costs and impact on economic development.

In particular, DG V of the Commission focused on three main areas: the social implications of other programmes, such as agriculture, transport and regional policy; encouragement of employment and training policies, or the supply side of the labour market; and work designed to improve living and working conditions through studies.

Yet the Hague summit in 1969 placed a new emphasis on the need for a proactive social policy, especially 'the political acceptance of social goals' (Collins, 1975). The Summit acknowledged the positive role of the European Social Fund, requested the Commission to conduct new studies on social security and led to the creation of the Standing Committee on Employment (which brings together the Commission, Council and social partners into one forum). The third medium-term economic programme, adopted by the Council in February 1971, and the preliminary guidelines for a Community social policy programme submitted by DG V the following month, placed economic and social policy on an equal footing.

The reasons for this shift in opinion - towards more general support for social policy - are complex, but include growing awareness of the unevenness of growth across the member states, with the peripheral areas lagging more and more behind the richer ones; awareness of the continuing exclusion of certain groups - such as women and disabled people - from the labour market; and the effects of the structural revolution brought about by the common market itself (Shanks, 1977, pp. 4-5).

To these points - which have been repeated in the 1980s and 1990s to justify the creation of the EC's 'social dimension' to accompany the single European market - we could add the significance of political events in France, where de Gaulle had fallen in 1969, and in West Germany where, the same year, Willy Brandt had formed a new Social Democratic Government. Moreover, it was increasingly clear that enlargement of the Six to embrace three new members - Denmark, the Republic of Ireland and the UK, whose accession took effect from 1 January 1973 - also required fresh orientations in social policy.

So it was that, in October 1972 at the Paris summit, heads of state and government of the EC member states invited the Commission, in consultation with the other EC institutions and social partners, to draw up a social action programme.

Stage 2: 1972-1980

The social action programme was adopted by a resolution in 1974 and contained around 40 initiatives grouped under three principal objectives: full and better employment, improved living and working conditions and worker participation (Shanks, 1977).

Indeed, analysis of the measures proposed by DG V during this second stage in the development of EC social policy - with the oil shocks, spiralling inflation and rising unemployment of the 1970s as the background - reveals concentration on a number of limited areas: employment protection, equal treatment for men and women, participation and health and safety at work.

Employment protection
One series of Directives attempted to protect workers' rights in the face of the recession. The 1975 Directive on collective redundancies covered rights to information and consultation when redundancies were planned, whilst the 1977 Directive on the transfer of undertakings guaranteed the continuity of employees' contractual and statutory rights in cases of mergers and takeovers, as well as certain rights to information and consultation before the transfer takes place. The 1980 insolvency Directive protected workers' pay if their company ceased trading.

Employee participation
Undoubtedly one of the most difficult areas has been the introduction of employee participation into large enterprises. Proposed legislation has focussed chiefly on representational participation at board level or on information disclosure and consultation in companies with complex structures (though a third kind, financial participation, has now also been proposed through a Recommendation on the promotion of employee participation in profits and enterprise results (PEPPER), adopted by the Council in June 1992.

During the period under review, proposals were submitted for both a European Company Statute (1970) and a Fifth Directive on the structure of public limited companies (1972). The former would have required enterprises intending to register as a European Company to introduce employee representation on to their supervisory boards and to set up a European-level works council, whilst the latter would have required the introduction of a two-tier board structure, with employee representation on the supervisory board, in all companies with 500 or more employees.

No agreement was reached on either (though a revamped European Company Statute was proposed

in August 1989). Opposition from both employers and governments was based on a variety of factors - notably the alleged restrictive nature of the proposals (based chiefly on the German pattern) and the concern that the balance of power would be tipped in the unions' favour in the matter of corporate decision-making.

Equal treatment for men and women
Three major Directives on equal treatment were adopted during the second stage of EC social policy: the 1975 equal pay Directive, which required member states to ensure abolition of all pay discrimination and application of the principle of equal pay for work of equal value; the 1976 equal treatment Directive, which dealt with access to employment, promotion, vocational training and working conditions; and the 1978 Directive on equal treatment for men and women in state social security. A series of equality cases in the early 1970s, based on Article 119 of the EEC Treaty, had also been dealt with by the European Court of Justice, a process which had begun to bolster EC social policy through the addition of case law.

Health and safety
A number of health and safety Directives were also adopted during this stage - notably on the use of electrical equipment in potentially explosive atmospheres (1976) and on safety signs at the workplace (1977). However, greatest progress in this field did not take place until the 1980s, particularly following the extension of qualified majority voting on the Council to cover health and safety issues.

Stage 3: 1980-1987

Mixed fortunes characterise DG V's initiatives during the third stage in the development of EC social policy.

On the one hand, a number of significant Directives on health and safety were adopted, including those covering lead (1982), asbestos (1983) and noise (1986). In addition, several measures on equal treatment were adopted: the Recommendation on the promotion of positive action for women (1984), the Directive on equal treatment in occupational social security schemes (1986) and the Directive on equal treatment for the self-employed and the protection of self-employed women during pregnancy and motherhood (1986).

On the other hand, however, deadlock paralysed progress in other areas. Draft Directives on part-time work, temporary work, and parental leave and leave for family reasons were all stymied as were various miscellaneous measures including the

Recommendation on reduction and reorganisation of working time.

Attention focussed in particular on the failure of two major draft Directives to make progress - an amended version of the Fifth Directive, also referred to above, and the proposed 'Vredeling' Directive on procedures for informing and consulting employees in undertakings with complex structures (notably multinational companies).

The reasons for this slowdown in activity are complex. The most obvious is that the UK Government was willing to veto initiatives which it felt would raise labour costs and create rigidities on the labour market. The UK vigorously opposed the draft Directives on part-time work, temporary work, parental leave and information and consultation in multinationals. The UK also vetoed the draft Recommendation on reduction and reorganisation of working time at the Council meeting in June 1984 (Teague, 1989, pp. 66). Furthermore, during its 1986 Presidency, it secured the adoption of an Action Programme for Employment Growth which stressed the need for deregulation and flexibility in labour markets (Matthews, 1992).

Changing economic climate
However, the adoption of this Action Programme also partly reflects important changes in other EC member states, many of which, by the mid-1980s, either had right- or centre-right governments or else Socialist governments which had themselves adopted tight economic policies (notably France and Spain). In addition, deregulatory labour market policies had also become more widespread across a number of member states (Vranken, 1986).

Partly as a result of these changes, the interpretation of harmonisation in Article 117 as the 'partial alignment' of social policy was coming more and more to be questioned. This was not only because of the further enlargement of the EEC - Greece joined in 1980 and Spain and Portugal in 1986 - but also because record post-war levels of unemployment and the ever intensifying search for international competitiveness cast a shadow over the practicality of an interpretation which had been elaborated under very different economic circumstances.

The grounds for basing certain Directives - for example, the one on collective redundancies - on Article 100 of the Treaty, which governs the rights of the Council in relation to measures which 'directly affect the establishment or functioning of the common market', is that there are also clear cost implications of varying labour standards between member states. Those which impose higher standards, not just over redundancy procedures but also over other areas like equal pay and participation, are likely to face higher labour costs than those which do not, and hence competitive disadvantage. During the 1980s, certain governments came to see advantages in keeping labour costs down to ensure the efficient working of the economy, manufacture cheaper products and enhance competitiveness in general, whilst the Commission itself also came increasingly to the view that the EEC as a whole had to guard against spiralling labour costs in order to maintain its edge against other international competitors (particularly in the Far East).

Subsidiarity
Out of such considerations evolved the concept of 'subsidiarity' - the notion that the EC should involve itself only in those areas which cannot be dealt with more efficiently at national level (Spiker, 1991) and where the proposed action would help reach a Community objective. This concept therefore stresses the inappropriateness of EC-wide legislation in, for example, the context of widely varying regulatory frameworks between member states. In this respect, it has been pointed out that collective rights are more difficult to harmonise than individual rights - employees' rights to information and consultation, for instance, cannot be divorced from the industrial relations contexts in each country, such as the role of law, the significance of trade unions, the existence of statutorily based works councils, and so on, all of which involve controversial areas for debate.

The problem is that 'subsidiarity' has had no clear legal meaning. Until its definition in Article 3b of the new Treaty on European Union signed in February 1992 the term had not been mentioned in the EEC Treaty at all, and so it often appeared to be invoked to justify ad hoc political stances. But it had come to eclipse the notion of partial alignment as the guiding principle for social policy in the EC in the 1980s, and this position has now been consolidated in the new Treaty.

Social dialogue
As the legislative approach began to falter, the Commission also reactivated a specific process of consultation between itself and employers' and union organisations at the European level - a process known as the 'social dialogue'. A network of European-level committees bringing together both sides of industry and services had existed for years, the most important example being of course the Economic and Social Committee. However, in January 1985, the Commission set up a series of informal tripartite

contacts which culminated the following November at Val Duchesse outside Brussels. This meeting, which discussed economic growth and employment, led to a more formalised system of working parties covering areas like macroeconomic policy and new technology. Since then, sector-level social dialogue has also developed - discussions have led to a series of joint opinions, focussing mainly on training, agreed between European-level employers and unions at sector level in retailing, construction, energy supply amongst others.

Promotion of the social dialogue has been one of the Commission's responsibilities since 1987 (under Article 118B of the amended EEC Treaty) and, indeed, such is the importance attached to this process that DG V - the Directorate-General concerned with employment, industrial relations and social affairs - has been internally reorganised to reflect the new priorities: unit A1 deals with social dialogue and unit A2 with social dialogue at sector level.

Under the terms of Article 4 of the Social Protocol appended to the new Treaty on European Union, the social dialogue has been enhanced in a variety of ways, perhaps even paving the way for eventual Community-level collective bargaining (though excluding the UK which did not sign the Protocol). Further ways to encourage this process are contained in the Commission's White Paper, *European Social Policy - A Way forward for the Union* (Commission of the EC, 1994a: Section VIII).

Social cohesion
Cohesion has been defined in principally economic rather than social terms. Much attention has been devoted, especially since 1987, to the need to reduce regional disparities (clearly a serious problem in view of the probable enlargement of the EC in coming years).

However, little attention, until recently, has been focused on social cohesion or the notion of solidarity or citizenship. It is true that the Treaty provides for an Economic and Social Committee consisting of 'representatives of the various categories of economic and social activity', notably producers, farmers, workers and the professions (Article 193). This Committee, which has an advisory function, must be consulted as laid down in the Treaty. But this hardly affects social cohesion in the general sense. Since 1987, only Article 118B - as we saw in the preceding section - has referred to the role of the 'social dialogue' in promoting 'relations based on agreement' between management and labour at EC-level. Otherwise, whilst DG V has some responsibility for poverty programmes and education (Commission

of the EC, 1994: Section VI), it has none at all for other major areas of social policy like housing. And it is only now, in the Treaty on European Union, that a start has been made on tackling the difficult areas of citizenship and the voting rights of EC nationals residing in another member state.

Stage 4: 1987 to the present - the Social Action Programme White Paper

The current stage in the development of EC social policy began with the Belgian Presidency of the Council of Ministers in the first half of 1987. Acknowledging implicitly the problems associated with the harmonisation of social policy in terms of upwards or partial alignment, the Presidency proposed the adoption of an EC-wide platform of guaranteed minimum social rights in an attempt to revitalise the political initiative in this area.

After much debate within the institutions of the EC and amongst the social partners, the Community Charter of the Fundamental Social Rights of Workers - the Social Charter - was adopted at the Strasbourg summit in December 1989 by eleven of the twelve EC member states (excluding the UK and prior to the accession of Austria, Finland and Sweden). It was adopted as a 'solemn declaration' but required the Commission to set out a social action programme to accompany it. The action programme itself proposed 47 separate initiatives related to the Social Charter, each one to follow its own path through the necessary procedures. Overall, the Social Charter steered a course between 'upwards harmonisation' on the one hand and the 'hands off' non-interventionist approach advocated by the UK on the other. This is also the course adopted by the Commission's White Paper that states:

'Continuing social progress can be built only on economic prosperity, and therefore on the competitiveness of the European economy. The key to this is continuing productivity gains...' (Commission of the EC, 1994 para. 17, p. 4) and

'Minimum standards are needed to preserve the cohesion of the Union, having regard to differing national systems and needs, and to the relative economic strengths of the different Member States. The establishment of a framework of basic minimum standards...provides a bulwark against using low social standards as an instrument of unfair economic competition...' (Commission of the EC, 1994a para. 19, p. 5)

Social Policy and the Social Charter

The Commission's action programme, published in November 1989 to accompany the Social Charter, seemed to herald a new era of interventionism in the social policy arena. However, this observation needs to be hedged with a number of reservations.

First of all, the amended EEC Treaty - in introducing qualified majority voting to encourage 'improvements, especially in the working environment, as regards the health and safety of workers' (Article 118A) - had already prompted a wave of new Directives on health and safety. Given that unanimity on the Council was no longer required, the Commission had proposed in February 1988 a framework Directive on health and safety along with six individual or 'daughter' Directives within its remit. A couple more soon followed - on carcinogens and biological agents - well before the Social Charter was finalised.

Secondly, disagreements over the direction of labour market policy persist, and to these have been added controversy over the legal basis for certain measures. For example, the Directive on working time has been contested on the grounds that it deals with employment rights rather than health and safety and so should have been introduced under Article 100A of the Treaty rather than Article 118A.

Thirdly, the social action programme itself lacks overall coherence. Far from representing an attempt to define systematically a set of social rights - as is the case with the Council of Europe's Social Charter, for example - the programme reflects a pragmatic approach on the part of the Commission. Given the lack of genuine consensus over the direction of social policy and the complexity of the procedures required to adopt EC legislation, the Commission has opted for what might be described as a 'bolt-on' approach. Since a coherent set of social rights is not considered as an essential precondition for the economic success of the single European market, they have come to be seen in certain quarters as an 'extra', an 'aside' from the real business of the EC which is all about growth, competitiveness and markets.

As a result of this, the 47 or so proposals contained in the social action programme may be characterised as follows:

- Updates of existing measures (such as the 1975 redundancies Directive and the 1983 asbestos Directive);

- Incorporation of measures already in progress (such as several of those under the headings of labour market, like the 'Employment in Europe Report' and the action programmes on employment creation for specific target groups, and vocational training, like certain exchange programmes);

- Revamping of certain deadlocked measures (such as those on 'atypical workers' and the European Works Councils, which grew at least partly out of the draft Directive on part-timers and 'Vredeling' respectively);

- Certain genuine new measures (such as those concerning posted workers, maternity leave, financial participation and health and safety of workers on temporary and mobile work sites).

In partial explanation of this last point, the Commission set out its proposals in line with the principle of subsidiarity - that is, in line with the principle that the EC acts only when it can attain its objectives more effectively at its own level than that of its member states. This meant that in some cases, the Commission did not propose any initiatives at all despite their inclusion in the Social Charter (such as freedom of association and the right to collective bargaining).

In other cases, the Commission restricted its proposals to a non-binding Recommendation or Communication (as in areas like social protection, child care, an equitable wage or rights of workers living in frontier regions). The Commisson considered that such matters should be left either to national or regional action by member states or to the two sides of industry. However, in view of certain common aspects of these problems which affect most if not all of the member states, the Commission has indicated how best they might be tackled in an attempt to secure the maximum possible degree of convergence.

Finally, the Commission has been criticised for protecting the interests of the employed and the organised at the expense of the unemployed, the young, elderly and disabled and temporary migrants from outside the EC. Some of these criticisms are undoubtedly valid, though headings in the action programme do cover all these categories of citizen. In addition, it must be borne in mind that certain key areas of social policy - such as housing - fall outside its competence altogether as defined by the EEC Treaty.

IV The Maastricht Summit

Throughout 1991 - following a decision at the European Council in Rome in December 1990 - two sets of Intergovernmental Conferences (IGCs) ran parallel, one on economic and monetary union, the other on political union. These culminated at the European Council in Maastricht in December 1991 in agreement on two Treaties, a Treaty on Economic and Monetary Union and a Treaty on Political Union respectively. The text of the two Treaties was subsequently merged and formally signed by the heads of state and government on 7 February 1992. The merged text is known as the Treaty on European Union. This Treaty constitutes the second set of constitutional amendments to the 1957 EEC Treaty, the first being the Single European Act, which came into force in July 1987. The new Treaty on European Union, like the Single European Act, would introduce significant procedural and substantive changes into the operations of the EC (further revisions to the EEC Treaty are scheduled for discussion in 1996).

All the amendments insofar as the social dimension is concerned are concentrated into the Treaty on Political Union. Social policy had been widely regarded as one of the more serious obstacles standing in the way of a successful outcome. Of the other two perceived obstacles, Spain's demands for larger amounts of 'cohesion' money were largely conceded, whilst the second, the UK's objections to reference to 'a federal goal' in the preamble to the Treaty on Political Union, was sidestepped by referring instead to its marking a new stage in the creation of 'an ever closer Union among the peoples of Europe', a phrase which already exists in the EEC Treaty.

In a final attempt to secure agreement, the Social Chapter in the Treaty remained unchanged but with the exception of the UK member states adopted their own agreement of social policy to allow them , should they wish to take action in the social policy area without the UK. (However, the precedent for a 'two-speed Europe' had been set in June 1990 when the Schengen Convention - which aims to facilitate free movement of people between the signatory states - was signed by the Benelux countries, France, Germany and Italy (and since by Portugal and Spain.)

The resulting final text of the Treaty on European Union, which contains a series of protocols, therefore includes the Protocol on Social Policy, to which is annexed a separate agreement (since January 1995 Austria, Finland and Sweden are also parties to the Treaty and the Protocol).

- The Protocol on Social Policy notes that 'eleven member states...wish to continue along the path laid down in the 1989 Social Charter' and so exempts the UK from participation in the Agreement annexed to it.

- An 'Agreement on social policy concluded between the member states of the EC with the exception of the UK' contains what had been intended to be the social chapter itself, that is, the amended versions of EEC Treaty Articles 117 to 122.

Protocol on Social Policy

The original intention at the Maastricht summit, as we saw above, was to replace the principal social policy Articles of the EEC Treaty with a new social chapter. Eleven member states agreed these amendments as presented by the Dutch Presidency, the most controversial of which extended qualified majority voting to cover adoption of measures relating to working conditions and information and consultation of workers, and promoted contractual relations between employers and employees at European level. However, none of the amendments was accepted by the UK Government.

The eventual Protocol on Social Policy states that the eleven 'have adopted among themselves' an Agreement to continue along the path laid down in the 1989 Social Charter and that the contracting parties, including of course the UK -

'Agree to authorise those eleven member states to have recourse to the institutions, procedures and mechanisms of the European Community for the purposes of taking among themselves and applying as far as they are concerned the necessary decisions.'

The Protocol adds that the UK 'shall not take part in the deliberations and the adoption by the Council of Commission proposals made on the basis of this Protocol and the above-mentioned Agreement'. Proposals requiring a qualified majority vote will therefore be adopted if they receive 44 out of a possible 66 votes (rather than 54/76, when the UK is included). Those requiring unanimity will still require unanimity, but amongst the eleven only.

So the question now naturally arises: what are the practical implications of having two means of taking forward social policy?

First, the Commission will continue to plan the implementation of the social action programme on the basis of full agreement of all fifteen member states (including, since January 1995, Austria, Finland and Sweden) as prior to the Treaty on European Union. However, if a proposal is blocked because of opposition from the UK, then the Commission has recourse to its second set of procedures laid out under the Social Protocol. The other fourteen may then take their own decisions outside the Treaty and, as the Commission itself puts it, such 'agreements made under the Protocol will still be taken within the framework of the Community's institutions 'on loan' to the Protocol signatory states' (Commission of the EC, 1992c).

The first procedure, then, remains located within the familiar, existing provisions of the Treaty, whilst the second is located outside, as a kind of private arrangement amongst the fourteen but with the agreement of the UK. Because the EEC Treaty continues to bind all parties, the Commission have said that they will introduce proposals under the Treaty first before using the Protocol.

Indeed, the first test for this new procedure was the draft European Works Councils Directive, which was introduced under the second procedure noted above. Political agreement on a 'common position' was reached under the Greek Presidency in June 1994, and final adoption took place in September 1994 under the German Presidency (Gold and Hall, 1994). Furthermore, the Commission stated that if progress on the draft Posted Workers Directive was not made by the end of 1994, then it would consider consultations with the social partners under the social protocol (Commission of the EC, 1994a, p. 21-22).

The UK position

The important point to bear in mind when assessing the UK's position is that the UK is, of course, still bound by the existing Articles of the EEC Treaty relating to social policy.

Conclusion

From the very inception of the European Communities, the relationship between the Commission and the member states has been fraught, not least as regards the development of social policy. The Commission, in its attempts to ensure basic social and labour rights across the member states, has interpreted its responsibilities in a broadly interventionist sense, though by the late 1980s a less interventionist approach to these issues had become increasingly widespread. The member states themselves, by contrast, have always shown concern over what they have sometimes perceived as an erosion of their powers by the Commission. This concern has been greatest in the UK which, in 1991, chose to stay out of the binding process towards the alignment of social policy by signing the Social Protocol to the Maastricht Treaty.

Footnote on Section 1

1. Observers agree on the dates of the first stage, 1958-72, but disagree over the markers for the subsequent stages. For example, Hepple (1981) has 1972-80 ('social action') and since 1980 ('crisis and deregulation'), whilst Bridgford and Stirling (1991) have 1972-84 ('interventionist') and 1985-1990 ('contradictory trends'). Brewster and Teague (1989), on the other hand, have 1973-83 and post 1983. This section follows Hepple in seeing 1980 as a turning point, but also consider 1987 - the year the Single European Act came into force - as another.

Section 2
Formulation of
EC Social Policy

Policy - to be defined as policy at all - must be developed and formulated. Once formulated, it can be implemented, watered down, ignored, enforced or just plain forgotten and indeed all these processes have been widely analysed by commentators. But a question remains: how is policy formulated at the earliest, embryonic phase, before it is eventually drafted and published?

The answer, insofar as policy based on agreement is concerned, is that it is the outcome of negotiations between the relevant parties. The parties draw up their own objectives, demands and fall-back positions and, assuming all goes well, an outcome acceptable to all parties is reached.

However, the origins of draft legislation within the Commission are more complex. Clearly, decisions must be taken about the general areas in which policy is to be generated, whilst the surrounding issues must be clarified and the general orientation established. Though all these processes might involve written material - memos, discussion documents and so on - none of it will normally be made public. It will remain internal to the organisation until the final version of the draft instrument is published. At this point only does the policy become the object of attention and lobbying. Only then, after all, does it have form and content and therefore the status to become an object for discussion, criticism, amendment, adoption and so on. Lobbyists are obliged to bring pressure to bear around the parameters which have already been set.

The question, then, is how these policy parameters are in fact set. At one level, of course, the answer is clear. Policy-making processes are laid down in the Treaties, which entitle the various EC institutions to initiate, enact and monitor legislation and establish the procedures by which this is to be accomplished. In the words of one constitutional authority:

> 'The powers of the Community to take legislative or executive action are granted by various provisions in the Treaties, and the procedure which must be followed in the exercise of these powers depends on the particular provision in question'
> (Hartley, 1986).

In this respect, for all practical purposes, the initiation of EC policy lies with the Commission as a body. Article 155 of the Treaty states:

> 'In order to ensure the proper functioning and development of the common market, the Commission shall...have its own power of decision... [and] exercise the powers conferred on it by the Council for the implementation of the rules laid down by the latter.'

A series of further Articles then specify the areas in which the Commission may issue proposals and the nature of the voting procedures on the Council required for their adoption, namely whether it must act on a unanimous vote or a qualified majority vote.[1]

However, at another level, this legalistic explanation of the formulation of EC policy still leaves a tale to be told. Even though we can establish that the Commission has the power necessary to initiate policy, a crucial question remains: how does a draft instrument acquire its *specific* content? That is, how does the Commission convert its power to initiate policy into detailed proposals containing this set of provisions rather than that?

For example, in late 1989 the Commission adopted the social action programme (Commission of the EC, 1989) then containing some 47 proposals designed to implement the Social Charter (Commission of the EC, 1992) which had been endorsed by eleven of the twelve member states at the Strasbourg summit the previous December. This action programme laid down the broad policy objectives of the Commission for the three years 1990, 1991 and 1992 and so defined the scope of the agendas of Councils of Social and Labour Ministers over that period. It is not difficult to observe the relationship between the Social Charter on the one hand and the Social Action Programme on the other.

Yet the Social Action Programme refers to each of the 47 proposals in just a few paragraphs. There is little to indicate the nature of the final proposals as released by the Commission in the form of a draft Directive, Recommendation or whatever and still less to indicate the likely impact on member states of their enactment. Yet many of the proposals were wide-ranging, covering significant and by now familiar areas like working time, the conditions of atypical workers, collective redundancies and so on.

Many of the studies focusing on Community decision-making say very little about the process through which policy objectives are turned into actual, detailed initiatives or proposals. The purpose of this chapter is to examine this process in relation to three of these social action programme initiatives: the European Works Council Directive; the collective redundancies Directive; and the Recommendation on the promotion of employee participation in profits and enterprise results (PEPPER).

Current studies on decision-making
First, however, we need to look more closely at the principal characteristics of decision-making in the EC as revealed in a number of current studies.

- Emphasis centres on official or constitutional procedures: a standard description of the decision-making process within the EC will refer to the competence of the principal EC institutions and their relationships in terms of formal bureaucratic procedures (see for example Borchardt, 1990; Ludlow, 1991). Explanations are frequently couched in static or legal terms, much in the manner outlined at the start of this paper. Where change is alluded to, it is often seen as the result of constitutional amendment, such as the introduction of the Single European Act (and, for example, extension of the 'co-operation procedure' to a wider range of social policy areas).

- Emphasis, as a result, tends to focus on the later stages of policy formulation: whilst many commentators discuss the role of the Economic and Social Committee, the European Parliament, COREPER and the Council in EC policy formulation at some length (see for example Freestone & Davidson, 1988), few stress the critical stage at which the formulation of the first draft of a new instrument takes place (an exception is Budd, 1987). Those who do, as we shall maintain later, do not always grasp the fluidity of the processes involved.

- Emphasis is placed on the established role of lobby groups: attention has been directed principally towards the publicly observable activity of pressure groups, particularly the social partners, with rather less on the 'behind the scenes' lobbying of the other major actors at EC level, national governments (for a recent review of developments see Mazey & Richardson, 1992).

Implicit model
There is a model implicit in these emphases on official channels, the later stages of policy formulation and observable lobbying activity.

Bachrach and Baratz (1970), in a classic study, draw a distinction between two faces of power, which is revealing in this context. In a critique of the concept of power developed by a number of US pluralist writers, Bachrach and Baratz note that they focus exclusively on the study of observable behaviour, on decision-making as a process and on instances of conflict over specific issues. So for example such pluralists would suggest that power lay with those individuals or groups whose interests prevailed in conflicts over identifiable issues. Such a view, argue Bachrach and Baratz, is one-sided, as it leaves out of account another facet of power, namely the ability to prevent certain issues from arising in the first place (non-decision making). This requires the identification of potential issues which non-decisions prevent from becoming 'real'. Lack of conflict does not, therefore, necessarily imply consensus, but rather - perhaps - that it is successfully being kept covert rather than overt.

It would seem that this debate throws some light on the study of decision-making within the EC. Emphasis on official channels, and analysis of the behavioural aspects of power - the outcome of meetings, changes in the wording of draft legislation, the adoption of resolutions and so on - , is very much in line with the first face of power criticised by Bachrach and Baratz. Of equal, or greater interest, is the study of the ways in which agendas are set and issues are presented in one form rather than another in line with dominant interests and perspectives. This might involve the study of informal processes within, for example, the Commission, particularly the formation and maintenance of social networks responsible for giving acceptable advice, interaction with certain pressure groups rather than others, the holding of informal meetings without minutes and the passing over of views which do not fit in with prevailing assumptions.

Such an approach would, of necessity, focus on the very earliest stages of policy initiative-taking. This is because the process through which, say, a draft Directive comes to be phrased in one way rather than another - or stresses, or fails to stress, certain aspects rather than others - is critical in determining the parameters of subsequent debate. To take but one example: the Commission determined in its social action programme that there should be a Community instrument on the procedures for the information, consultation and participation of the workers of European-scale undertakings. Its choice of a works council structure at the pre-drafting stage effectively ruled out debate around other possible forms of information/consultation arrangement at EC level.[2]

Finally, this approach would also explain some of the tensions which exist between the Commission on the one hand and national governments on the other. The supranational nature of the Commission as well as its close ties with the social partners, especially the unions, have always led to concern on the part of the governments of the member states. The attempts made by the Commission to interpret Articles 117 and 118 in a broad sense favourably to itself led to problems from the outset. Even in the early 1960s, one commentator noted:

> '[The Commission] was attacked for its actions in choosing subject matter [for studies under Article 118] not previously approved by governments or which went beyond the scope of the Treaty, in making direct contacts with non-public authorities and for the creation of committees not directly specified by the Treaty.... All such moves by the Commission [to create committees] suggested that governments might be bypassed and action encouraged which was unwelcome to them'
> (Collins, 1975).

This quotation reveals an awareness on the part of national governments of the crucial importance of the early stages of EC policy formulation. In each case there is concern that the Commission has access to a form of power which gives it an early advantage over the interests of national governments. Here we have called this acknowledging the second face of power, but it could also be termed the power to control agendas or, indeed, more graphically, as 'shooting where the ducks are'. Mazey and Richardson (1992) use this expression to summarise the way in which interest groups 're-target their influence, once they realise that the power to take decisions which affect them has moved to a new institution or to new actors'. As we shall show later on, the UK Government - at least in relation to social policy - has become increasingly concerned not only to influence agendas but to be involved in the progress of policy from its inception.

It is therefore not surprising, in view of the struggle between governments and the Commission both over perceived erosions of sovereignty and over the general direction of different aspects of EU policy that this concern to influence policy at the earliest possible stages should result in a degree of tension. It certainly raises major issues of accountability.

It is perhaps more surprising that it has received rather scant attention in the literature, though some reasons can be advanced for this, notably the difficulty of gaining access to reliable information in an area characterised by informal networks and confidentiality. In some cases we know something about policy formulation before the adoption of a formal proposal as there do indeed exist formal channels - for example in health and safety.[3] In other cases, an unofficial procedure may become official - as we shall see below, the process of 'social dialogue' revived by Jacques Delors in 1985 culminated in an agreement in January 1989 which permitted the social partners formally to request early consultations over policy formulation which hitherto had been carried out informally. This, of course, makes such procedures more transparent. However, in yet other cases, it is possible to make progress in unravelling the complexity of the processes involved only through the art of conversation, informal interviews and corroborating the facts as accurately as possible.

To return, then, to the main aim of this chapter: this is to examine the early formulation of social and labour initiatives in the EC, notably that prior to the publication of a draft instrument. We can distinguish two stages in this process:

first, preparation of a text, for example, in terms of research, contacts and so on; and

secondly, once the first draft of a text has been drawn up, the period of lobbying within the Commission pre-publication, that is, the process of consultation before a revised version is published as the official draft Directive or Recommendation.

Only then is the proposal submitted to the other institutions of the EC, notably the Council, but also to the Economic and Social Committee and European Parliament for their Opinions. However, by then, the proposal is very much in the public domain and so falls outside the remit of this paper.

Preparation

As far as the preparation of a text is concerned, a standard description, reflecting very much the pluralist assumptions outlined above, runs as follows:

> 'The first stage in the normal decision-making process consists of the formulation of the Commission proposal. A working group is formed, made up of persons nominated by the national governments, who are usually civil servants but sometimes academics or other independent experts. The powers of the group are only advisory: at this stage the final decision rests with the Commission; but the views of the national experts are listened to very carefully, since the consent of the national governments will have to be obtained at a later stage. After the working group has held a number of meetings and careful consideration has been given to the opinions of the national governments and appropriate non-governmental

groups (for example, the relevant trade associations) the Commission will draft its proposal' (Hartley, 1986).

Clearly, practice may vary between Directorates-General in the Commission, but although this account was probably a fair description of DG III and DG XV at the time, insofar as it refers to DG V is inaccurate on several points. A working group is not always formed; its members are not necessarily nominated by national governments; nor are they 'usually civil servants' (at least in the cases analysed in this paper); and 'careful consideration' has not necessarily - until recently - been given to the opinions of the national governments. Finally, perhaps most importantly, the impression that there is one, unbending framework for policy formulation at the early stages is misleading. Rather, the approach is fluid and pragmatic, reflecting the very real constraints under which the Commission operates.

An analysis of some case studies, drawn principally from the Social Action Programme, helps to illustrate this fluidity and pragmatism.

The Social Action Programme, based on the Social Charter, established the broad areas on which the Commission was required to publish proposals over the three years 1990-92. For many of them, the Commission requires a working paper or some other foundation on which to base its eventual proposal. Since the Commission is not as vast a bureaucracy as is often supposed, it does not normally have the staff to deal with this preparation in-house (indeed, it frequently recruits staff on fixed-term contracts or secondments to assist permanent staff on particular topics).

This preparation can be an immensely complex affair, since the Commission has to have an up-to-date overview of the current situation prevailing in relation to its chosen proposal (such as working time, redundancy procedures and so on) in each of the twelve member states before it can make any progress. This requires an understanding of diverse legal and social frameworks, material on which is frequently available only in the source language.

As a result, the Commission normally delegates responsibility either to a working party or to an individual (often an academic) to carry out the initial spadework. For example, the first edition of the PEPPER Report was written by three experts, under Milica Uvalic of the European University Institute, along with contributions presented by participants from each member state to a Workshop held in May 1990.

On the other hand, reliance is sometimes placed on individuals. Preparatory work for the directives on transfers of undertakings and on collective redundancies was carried out by two academic labour lawyers well known in the UK and Belgium respectively. Similarly, the initial report which served as the basis for the draft Recommendation and Code of Practice on Sexual Harassment was drawn up by a lawyer with acknowledged expertise in this area. In his case, he had had little contact with the DG V of the Commission when asked to write the report, though he had already published articles on the subject in a variety of respected journals. In view of the American background to the issue, DG V apparently preferred an Anglophone rapporteur with easy access to English-language material, and a stagiaire (trainee) in the appropriate Directorate who knew the work of this particular expert made the approach, which was accepted.

The choice of method - working party or individual - depends partly on questions of timing and partly on the degree of clarity of the Commission's own ideas. It is generally quicker if an individual draws up the report, in addition to which the clearer the Commission is on what it wants, the easier it is to delegate a remit to an individual. A working party is more likely to come up with a range of ideas from which a proposal can be extracted.

However, some observations should be made about the remit itself and perceptions of it. UK civil servants have pointed out to NIESR that no attempt used to be made to assess the economic impact of a measure at this stage. For example, during the preparatory stages of the draft Directive on the protection of young people at work, submitted to the Council in March 1992, DGV did not, allegedly, know even how many young people would be covered, clearly a serious deficiency.

But there is a suspicion too that there is a set of assumptions about the content of eventual draft legislation even at the very start since, as it was put to the author, 'the cost of something has little to do with political requirements'. The view that social policy is determined through a process of 'political requirement' is, of course, true in the broad sense that the development of social policy is not merely a technical matter but one involving judgements about how - in this case - labour markets operate and how they affect issues like efficiency and distribution.

These perceptions illustrate the serious tensions that exist between diverging orientations towards social and labour policy: a non-interventionist market based approach one on the one hand which emphasises the need to create employment through reducing or eliminating constraints on labour markets; and a regulatory one on the other which emphasises, in contrast, the need to guarantee basic rights for the employed to prevent erosion of standards at work. Such divergences, and the mutual suspicion they tend to generate, may then magnify other factors and compound the problems - for example, the view that DGV takes 'a bit from this legislation and a bit from that' in drafting its proposals and that it pitches them high in order to establish a negotiating position later on.

Case 1: the European Works Council Directive
Sometimes, however, no preparatory work is directly carried out at all. In the case of the European Works Council (EWC) Directive, for example, the question was seen as an old one on which much work had already been completed.[4] The decision had been taken within Directorate A (Industrial Relations and Social Dialogue) of DGV that the works council approach was the one to take. Later on, DG V did commission research from the University of Warwick on the subject, but this was to help answer questions arising from the draft Directive itself - for example, the number of enterprises across the EC that would be affected by its provisions (Sisson, Waddington & Whitson, 1992). However, as the Memorandum to the draft Directive made clear, Commission staff did visit a number of multinationals - such as Bull and Pechiney - along with three main European Industry Committees in autumn 1990 to assess the current stage of development in voluntary systems of EWCs (Commission of the EC, 1991). This information fed into the framing of the draft Directive, but the civil servant responsible was otherwise shown the existing files, given his remit (a works council format) and allowed a week to produce the first version.

Once the first version was drafted, the process meshed in with the 'social dialogue'. The social dialogue, which had been launched by Jacques Delors in 1985 as a way of introducing a voluntarist element into the EC decision-making procedures, had acquired formal status in 1987 when the Single European Act took effect. Article 118B of the revised EEC Treaty states:

> 'The Commission shall endeavour to develop the dialogue between management and labour at European level which could, if the two sides consider it desirable, lead to relations based on agreement.'

One practical result of this was an agreement, concluded on 12 January 1989 at the Palais D'Egmont in Brussels, signed by the ETUC for the unions and UNICE and CEEP for the employers at EC-level.

It set up a tripartite steering group, chaired by the Commission, along with a couple of joint working parties designed to give the social dialogue a degree of continuity. One paragraph of the agreement ran:

> '[The steering group] will also be authorised to request the Commission to consult the two sides of industry on any project or proposal for a decision during its preparatory phase.'
> [emphasis added] (Commission of the EC, n.d.)

The procedure then developed as follows: the Commission produced a brief paper of one or two sides, known as a 'non-paper' or 'non-document', which outlined the proposal in question (though these have been criticised for being so general that it is impossible to identify the Commission's objectives). Proposals were paired: working time and atypical work were taken together; so were EWCs and proof of an employment contract; and later on - though by then the procedure had, as we shall see, changed somewhat - collective redundancies and PEPPER.

Meetings between the Commission and the social partners would last a day. One of the paired proposals would be taken in the morning, and the second in the afternoon. Each would be the only item on the agenda. ETUC, UNICE and CEEP would each make its comments, following which the Commission would revise its paper. One month to six weeks later, a second meeting would take place along the same lines, following which the Commission would finalise the text of the draft proposal.

These were not, of course, the only consultations going on prior to publication of the final draft Directive. Informal contacts were held bilaterally with the ETUC[5]) whilst labour lawyers were consulted over particular difficulties. Meanwhile, interested groups like the Institute of Personnel Management and the American Chamber of Commerce in Brussels were also already directing attention towards policy advisors to the Commissioner in relation to the EWC proposal. However, the shape of the eventual draft Directive was, by now, already fixed.

Lobbying within the Commission pre-publication

Once the Directorate - in this case Directorate A - together with the Director-General and possibly other DG V Directors is satisfied with the first draft, there are further stages to surmount within the Commission before the final version is released.

These stages provide an important pressure point for member states to lobby for amendments.

First, the proposal has to be studied and accepted by the Commissioner herself and her advisors (although in practice the cabinet has almost certainly been involved from the outset). The principal objection to the EWC draft at this stage was that it looked too long and threatening. However, an attempt to reduce the number of articles from 13 to six was successfully resisted internally.

Second, the accepted text along with its explanatory memorandum is circulated to all 23 Directorates-General. Each one has several days to register formal comments, though from the point of view of social and labour policy, only a few other DGs are important (notably DG III, Internal Market and Industrial Affairs, and DG XV, Financial Institutions and Company Law). In fact, DG XV lodged a complaint over the definition of a 'group' in the EWC text in relation to the definition already established in the draft European Company Statute, as a result of which changes were made to the former.

Third, the 20 *chefs de cabinet* (chief policy advisors of each Commissioner), together with special *chefs* and *attaches*, meet to examine the revised text along with full documentation. This meeting is fully minuted, and, as we shall see later, provides an opportunity to ambush a proposal through another DG.

Finally, the 20 Commissioners meet in similar fashion to endorse the revised text, and, all being well, the final version of the draft Directive or Recommendation is published around six weeks later.

Recent changes in pre-publication phase

We noted above that Vasso Papandreou, the former Commissioner responsible for social and labour affairs, had recently accepted proposals for 'improving Community legislation on social affairs'. The main effect was, to repeat the words of Michael Howard, the former Employment Secretary, 'to agree that experts from Member States' governments should be consulted before proposals are finalised by the Commission' (Employment Gazette, 1991).

In January 1991, Michael Howard had in fact approached Vasso Papandreou with two proposals: one was to introduce an impact assessment for all initiatives, whilst the other was to enhance the influence of national governments in the pre-publication phase. The interests of the government as regards the latter proposal were not only political, in

that it sought to amend or counter certain proposals which it opposed in principle, but also legal, in that it also hoped to improve the quality of the drafting.[6]

Indeed, in view of the consultations which the social partners could now request in line with the January 1989 agreement, it did seem one-sided to DG V to exclude the governments of the member states from a similar process. As a result, a new meeting, for representatives of member states, is often inserted between the two held for the social partners. To this meeting is circulated not a non-paper but an initial draft of the proposal in question, which is now also circulated to the second meeting of the social partners. In other words, the draft now begins to take shape even earlier - that is after the first meeting with the social partners but before the one with the governments of member states.

This process now governs the activities of at least DG V and DG XXIII, which is responsible for Enterprise Policy, Distributive Trades, Tourism and Co-operatives. In this way, representatives of the member states were involved in the formulation of the new draft Statutes for the European Association, a European Co-operative Society and a European Mutual Society, which are designed to complement the draft European Company Statute by providing an EC legislative framework for the non-profit making sectors of the economy.[7] These arrangements for consultations are fluid and may always be changed by the various Commission Directorate-Generals. A Vade Mecum on Commission procedure does exist for the use of Commission staff, but the authors have not seen a copy.

Case 2: collective redundancies
As we saw above, DG V has paired proposals for the purposes of consultation: the new consultative process involving national governments has so far covered collective redundancies and PEPPER. An analysis of each of these in turn reveals the extent to which 'non-decisions' - that is, aspects of the initiatives which have slipped through unchallenged - have been converted into issues by the governments through their abilities to intervene at earlier stages.

The Commission advocated the revision of the 1975 collective redundancies Directive in the light of the increasing rate of major transnational corporate restructuring across the EC resulting from the creation of the single European market. In the social action programme it argued that:

> 'A response at Community level appears the
> most appropriate approach especially since the
> Directive should apply in cases where the

decision concerning collective redundancies is taken by a decision-making centre or an undertaking located in another member state' (Commission of the EC, 1989, pp.20).

The original draft, as submitted to the consultation meeting with national governments, contained two points to which the UK objected. The first required company headquarters to transmit information about redundancies to local managements for disclosure to the worker representatives concerned in those cases where HQs were located in states other than where the redundancies were to take place. For example, a German company declaring redundancies in Belgium would have to transmit relevant details to the local management which would then be responsible for disclosing it to the Belgian works council. The second point required the designation of employee representatives to represent the workforce if there were none in enterprises with over 50 workers.

In the event, the amendment on the first point was adopted. Article 2(4) of the draft Directive now states that, in considering breaches of its requirements, 'account shall not be taken of any defence on the ground that the necessary information has not been provided by the undertaking which took the decision leading to collective dismissals'.

In relation to the second point, the draft Directive does not state unequivocally that member states must ensure the appointment of employee representatives so that its terms can be carried out. However, Article 2(5) states that 'member states need not provide for workers' representatives in respect of establishments normally employing less than 50 workers'.

The implication here is unclear: it could be that member states do need to provide for such representatives in establishments with a workforce above that threshold, though it could also mean that since no special provision is required in smaller establishments, provision in larger ones may be left to national legislation or practice.

Case 3: PEPPER
Initial research for Recommendation on the promotion of employee participation in profits and enterprise results (PEPPER) was carried out by Milica Uvalic of the European University Institute and two colleagues. A workshop on employee participation in company profits was held in May 1990, attended principally by academics (representatives of the member states were not invited). The first edition of the PEPPER report was then written incorporating the country studies presented at the workshop. The report was then submitted to a conference held in

Namur in October 1990, to which the member states were invited in order to make comments. Broadly speaking, this conference welcomed the report and pointed out any inaccuracies where they were found. A series of set speeches was made, covering issues like the relative merits of individual/collective schemes, statutory/voluntary-based schemes and so on. The UK argued successfully in favour of a draft Recommendation rather than a Directive, and lodged some criticisms over the prescriptive nature of the final chapter on the grounds that the format of a 'good scheme' varies in different circumstances. In this way, the Namur conference counts as a first informal consultation with the member states.

A revised edition of the PEPPER Report was then produced by March 1991, incorporating the observations made at Namur, and a preliminary draft Recommendation by May. The following month the second informal meeting between the member states and Commission took place, which resulted in a number of minor amendments to the text, such as a shorter preamble and the odd change of wording. In addition discussion centred on the role of the working party itself. The Commission intended to set it up to draw up a formula for PEPPER, but the member states, wary that the working party could be the precursor of unwelcome prescriptive legislation, did not wish to commit themselves to the terms of reference and composition of a working party within the confines of a Community instrument. They pointed out that the Commission did not need the authority of a Council Recommendation to set up a working party and that it would be preferable for the member states merely to take note of the Commission's intention to do so. The importance of this point lay in the fact that a number of problems remained in the application of PEPPER across the member states, partly because of varying tax regimes. In later discussion the reference to a working party was removed.

The Commission eventually adopted the text of the final draft in July 1991, and it was published the following September (Commission of the EC, 1991).

Conclusions

This chapter has highlighted the informality and fluidity of the processes involved in determining EC social initiatives in their early stages.

Even in the 1960s the Commission was criticised by member states for carrying out studies of topics, creating advisory committees and forging contacts with pressure groups in ways likely to expand its competence, so these aspects of its operations are not new. From the point of view of the Commission attempting to formulate policy across the width of the social dimension, however, this informality and fluidity is hardly surprising. The Commission has a task to fulfil, and, with limited resources or expertise in-house, it inevitably establishes links with outside experts who can assist sympathetically with its aims. For this reason, the names of certain 'tried and tested' individuals keep cropping up.

In the same way, the fluidity of the process meets the Commission's requirements. It can choose, on a pragmatic basis, whether to ask a working party or individual to assist in the preparation of an initiative, or indeed not to bother at all.

The informality and fluidity of these processes are in no small way determined by the very nature of the Commission's responsibilities within the framework of the EC. It is required to draw up instruments which are supranational in character and which therefore need to reflect the complexity of practice, traditions and legislation across fifteen quite diverse West European countries if they are to be at all workable. In order to meet that difficult objective it must ensure an 'open-door' approach by consulting extensively across the member states.

Not unnaturally such an approach concerns member states, especially when their political and social perspectives diverge from the broadly interventionist stance of the Commission. Well aware that once the Commission had released the text of a draft instrument its framework became much more difficult to influence, the UK government has successfully lobbied for the involvement of member states at an earlier stage of formulation as well as for assessments of the likely costs of implementing proposed legislation.

So far, these new procedures have affected principally measures concerning collective redundancies and PEPPER, but they have also been followed in relation to proposals governing the "economie sociale" - a set of three draft statutes drawn up by DG XXIII governing the non-profit making economy (such as associations, co-operatives and mutual societies). The extent to which these procedures become more generally applicable remains to be seen, but a number of questions arise. Once again, the raising of questions like these reveal the shifting, informal nature of the Commission which a purely formal or bureaucratic approach fails to explain.

Footnotes on Section 2

1. From the social affairs angle, the most important Articles are 49, 51, 54, 100, 100A, 118A and 235. Article 49 empowers the Council, in accordance with the Conciliation procedure involving the European Parliament, to issue directives on matters concerning 'freedom of movement for workers'. Article 51 allows the Council to adopt 'such measures in the field of social security as are necessary to provide freedom of movement for workers'. Article 54 allows the Council acting unanimously, in accordance with the Conciliation Procedure, to adopt measures for 'aboliton of existing restrictions on freedom of establishment'. Article 100 empowers the Council, acting on a unanimous vote on Commission proposals, to issue directives on matters concerning 'the establishment or functioning of the common market'. Article 100A allows the Council to act similarly but on a qualified vote on matters 'which have as their object the establishment and functioning of the internal market' (though exemptions cover fiscal policy, free movement of people and 'the rights and interests of employed persons'). Article 118A extends qualified majority voting principally to health and safety matters, whilst Article 235 grants the Council the right to act unanimously on matters not dealt with elsewhere if such action is required 'to attain … one of the objectives of the Community'.

2. The European Works Council is not mentioned as such in the Social Chapter, not even in chapter 7 of the social action programme, which states only that a Community instrument could follow a number of principles, of which one could be; 'Establishment of equivalent systems of worker representation in all European-scale enterprises'.

3. The Advisory Committee on Safety, Health and Hygiene, set up in 1974, consists of six representatives from each member state (that is, 72 in total), which two drawn equally from government, employers' organisations and unions. One of its responsibilities is to draw the attention of the Commission to areas for study and research.

4. 'Although in political terms the European Works Council Directive is the successor to Vredeling and was prepared by DG V, the proposal borrows from early versions of the European Company Statute by requiring the establishment of a specific company or group-level representative body – the European Works Council (Hall, 1992; see also Commission of the EC, 1975).

5. DG V's links with the trade unions have always been better than those with employers' organisations. This reflects greater agreement between the Commission and the unions over the aims of EC social policy – particularly in relation to interpretation of Article 117 - as well as the unions' superor organisation at EC-level for lobbying purposes.

6. Whilst no draft instrument may be submitted to the Commission without the approval of the Legal Service, there is no equivalent to the UK's Parliamentary Counsel, and so the subject experts responsible for drafting are not always experienced in this field of activity (see Gordon-Smith, 1989).

7. Official Journal C 99/92, 21 April 1992.

Section 3
Role of the Presidency

Following the previous section that analysed policy formulation in the early stages within the EC, this section examines the role of the Presidency in determining the final stages of social and labour policy. This aim is achieved through a case study of the 1986 UK Presidency.

Functions of the Presidency
The Presidency presents each member state in the rotating six month system with the opportunity to coordinate Community policy, set the agenda for Council meetings, and build consensus amongst the member states meeting within the Council. The powers of the Presidency are, however, extremely limited. Each member state holding the office faces severe time constraints imposed by the six month tenure. This problem is particularly acute where a member state holds the Presidency in the second half of the year, when the actual time available is much less than six months - a problem which has been addressed by Maastricht Treaty provisions which altered the order in which each member state holds the Presidency.

The Presidency is also constrained by its limited role and, unlike the Commission, has no powers of policy initiation enshrined in the EEC Treaty. This task remains with the Commission which, under Article 155 of the Treaty, formulates policy and proposes measures which then receive consideration by the European Parliament and the Council of Ministers, the latter which considers these proposals and adopts, amends or rejects them. The Council itself only possess the right to adopt resolutions on their own initiative. Resolutions have no binding force in Community law, and can be ignored by the Commission if it so wishes.

Similarly, the Presidency does not have any direct involvement in the policy implementation process. Once a decision is reached in the Council, implementation of Community policy becomes the responsibility of the Commission.

Despite the limitations imposed by the institutional framework of the Community, the UK Government used its 1986 Presidency of the Social Affairs Council to articulate an intergovernmental response to the problem of high levels of unemployment, which resulted in the adoption of a Resolution on an Action Programme on employment growth.

Origins of the initiative
The first concrete proposals of the Anglo-Irish-Italian initiative emerged on 28 May 1986 in the form of the document 'Employment Growth into the 1990s - A Strategy for the Labour Market', jointly submitted to the Council by the UK, Ireland and Italy.

The document was formally introduced by the UK at the Council meeting of 5 June 1986, towards the end of the Dutch Presidency (it is not clear whether the Dutch supported the document). The meeting was dominated by the decision to postpone further discussion of the draft Vredeling Directive until 1989 and by the impasse reached on the proposal for a directive on parental leave. A full consideration of the Anglo-Irish-Italian document was subsequently delayed until the Informal Meeting of EC Social Affairs Ministers in September, which would fall under the UK Presidency in the second half of 1986.

While the document contained many of the themes which had run through the Irish and Italian Presidencies, it also strongly reflected UK domestic policy, namely on the issues of deregulation, labour market flexibility and support for small firms. The originality of the document lay not in the specific proposals themselves, but more due to the fact that the member state holding the Presidency of the Council, with the support of two other member states, was determining both the pace and direction of Community social policy. In particular, the document was in sharp contrast to the Commission's Annual Economic Report for 1985-86, which had been adopted by the Council the previous year. The Annual Economic Report had used the Commission's emphasis on a cooperative growth strategy and the Social Dialogue as the basis for planned coordinated action to deal with the problem of unemployment at the Community level.

The general objective
The degree of difference evident between the approaches taken by the Commission's Annual Economic Report, with its emphasis on boosting investment and developing links with the social partners, and the Anglo-Irish-Italian document, with its emphasis on deregulation and flexible labour markets, is worthy of note. It illustrates clearly that the document which received support during the UK Presidency was only one of the approaches under consideration as a means of dealing with the problem of unemployment. The OECD, for example, had already begun negotiations at this time which resulted in adoption of the new Framework for Labour Market Policies, endorsed by all member states in 1990.

Where common ground did exist amongst the member states during this period was in a desire to deal with the unemployment issue in a systematic way at the Community level. This general objective goes some way towards explaining why the Anglo-Irish-Italian document received widespead support from other EC member states.

The Anglo-Irish-Italian Document
The Anglo-Irish-Italian initiative proposed action in four specific areas:

1. Promoting enterprise and employment by encouraging self-employment and small firms, including co-operatives;

2. Introducing flexible employment patterns and conditions of work by improving employment opportunities for women and ethnic minorities, encouraging employee share ownership, and facilitating intra-Community labour mobility, particularly through mutual recognition of qualifications;

3. Improving training provision, particularly youth training links with vocational education, and encouraging employers to invest in training;

4. Taking action to combat long-term unemployment, in particular through the provision of Social Fund support.

The initiative was significant in capturing the consensus of opinion at the time that new ideas and policies were needed to break the Community out of continued high levels of unemployment. It is for this reason more than any other that, at the Informal Meeting of EC Labour and Social Affairs Ministers in Edinburgh on 22-23 September 1986, the initiative received general support from Denmark, Germany and the Netherlands, despite disappointment with the text from the Irish and Italian ministers.

The Anglo-Irish-Italian initiative was somewhat of a departure from the established decision-making channels of the Community. Not only was it unusual for a proposal to come from the Member State holding the Presidency of the Council, supported by two other Member States, but the Council had throughout the first half of the 1980s either opposed or treated with extreme scepticism all Commission proposals relating to employment policy. The Anglo-Irish-Italian initiative was therefore highly unusual in that it proposed alternative policies to those put forward by the Commission, and appeared likely to be adopted despite the public criticism of the plan by Commissioner Manuel Marin, the European Parliament and the ETUC.

Reactions to the proposed Action Programme
At the Standing Committee on Employment meeting on 7 November 1986 there was some indication that a divergence of views existed on the most effective ways to fight unemployment.[1] However, despite some opposition from the ETUC, the meeting passed off amicably enough.

Hostility to the proposed Action Programme was more apparent in the European Parliament. On 11-12 November the plenary session of the European Parliament debated the conclusions of the Committtee on Social Affairs and Employment.[2] The debate revealed no support for the initiative apart from the British Conservative MEPs. The EP resolutions at the end of the debate, while not overtly condemning the Anglo-Irish-Italian initiative, called for a 'European Social Area' to be established, a framework directive establishing the fundamental rights of workers and adoption of the Vredeling Directive.[3] EP opposition to the initiative was interpreted by the UK government as an opportunity for various political groupings to voice their opposition to the policies of the Thatcher Government, and concern from MEPs that the proposed action programme would be a 'stalking horse' for the extension of UK domestic policies at an EC-wide level.

December 1986 Labour and Social Affairs Council meeting
On 11 December 1986 the employment and social affairs ministers of the twelve member states discussed the UK Presidency's draft resolution for an Action Programme on employment growth.

The proposed Resolution was adopted unanimously, after some amendments to make reference to the social dialogue and the strategy of cooperative economic growth, despite the misgivings of the Commission, and the criticisms of the Italian delegation.

Prior to the Social Affairs Council meeting, Commission vice-president Marin had said that the Commission would like the main themes in the cooperative growth strategy to be enhanced in the resolution, because although SMEs can create jobs, the main way of fighting unemployment is economic growth as it is described in the strategy. At the Labour and Social Affairs Council meeting, Commissioner Marin remained critical of the aim of increasing flexibility in the employment market on grounds that: 'There are currently millions of flexible contracts in the Community' and that the issue had already been dealt with sufficiently at the national level ('Europe' 12 December 1986). Marin instead suggested reinforcing the social dialogue on grounds that if the proceeds of growth are to be shared, it was better to do so equitably. Marin also pointed out that Italy, Portugal, Ireland and Spain all raised the basic problem of contributing financial means to the programme to combat unemployment, and questioned the validity of a programme without financial means.

Italy in particular, one of the original proponents of the Action Programme, was disappointed with the final Resolution, on grounds that it did not fulfil the intentions of the European Council declaration the previous week, nor the original motives behind the plan. De Michelis is reported ('Europe' 12 December 1986) to have urged a rapid implementation of concrete proposals because the Social Affairs Council had been discussing unemployment for three years and no progress had been made. De Michelis also submitted to his colleagues the outline of a proposal to create a Community Fund for employment development which reiterates his proposals of 1985. He proposed the creation of a special section of the European Social Fund or, alternatively, making an ad hoc fund financed by member states in proportion to the number of unemployed persons involved in intervention programmes. Each member state would have the right to use the fund in proportion to the number of unemployed persons, this creating jobs through internal spending programmes such as investment in infrastructure, research, and training programmes.

Other member states, however, were not willing to propose allocating extra resources to finance the Action Programme. The intention was that the Programme envisaged by the Resolution would be carried out with the Commission's existing resource base. Consequently, the final version of the Resolution concluded:

'The Council requests the Commission, within the available resources, to take into account the possibilities of helping the implementation of this Programme in its decisions on the various Community financial instruments....' [emphasis added].

Commission follow-up action

Report on the follow-up
The Commission published the first report on the follow-up to the Council Resolution on an Action Programme on employment growth on 10 November 1987,[4] eleven months after the Resolution was adopted. Part V of the Resolution of 22 December 1986, had invited the Commission to provide a written summary report on the progress made in implementing the Programme and on future developments every six months .[5]

Commentators on the Commission's response to the Resolution for an Action Programme noted a counter-strategy on the part of DG V in its first report on initiatives taken in accordance with the Resolution (see in particular Teague, 1989, pp. 73). Certainly it cannot be said that the emphasis of the Action Programme was reflected in the follow-up. Rather the Commission classified the Action Programme initiatives broadly within the framework of existing Community activities.

Examining the follow-up report in detail and comparing its content with that of the Council Resolution, particular patterns begin to emerge in the Commission's responses.

The Commission response
An analysis of the Commission follow-up report on the Council Resolution reveals a complex web of policy initiatives which may be roughly divided into the following categories:

(i) Where the Commission remained silent
It is extremely difficult to pinpoint those issues on which the Commission remained silent. The implication of silence would be that the Commission had failed to act on a particular objective set out in the Resolution. While the follow-up report gives the general impression that the aims and objectives of the Resolution were acted on, a small number of areas are discernible where no Commission response can be observed. The clearest example of Commission silence is its lack of response to calls made in the Resolution for measures to increase the number of persons, particularly young people and the unemployed, going into self-employment.[6]

(ii) Where action was taken by the Commission
The fact that the Commission's follow-up report was not published until November 1987, eleven months after the Resolution was adopted, allowed a considerable amount of time for action to be taken by the Commission in those areas highlighted by the Council (there is no evidence, however, of when the report was actually written). It is perhaps all the more surprising, then, that so little activity appears to have taken place over that eleven month period.

(a) In some cases *incorporation* into existing programmes took place. For example, in relation to *training* the Resolution had called for: more effective vocational programmes of education and training for young people; an increase in the prospects of young people leaving training; an increase in the levels of training and retraining opportunities available to adults; Community action to overcome restrictions on access to training, identification of training needs.

In its reponse to this part of the Resolution the Commission reported that it had adopted a draft Decision on the training and preparation of young people for adult working life in March 1987, a Communication on adult training in firms in January 1987, and a Communication on vocational training for women on 31 March 1987.

While these initiatives, all introduced after the December 1986 Resolution, were clearly in line with the broad principles laid down by the Council, it remains unclear to what extent Commission activity was *directly* prompted by the Resolution. For example, it would appear likely that Commission proposals adopted in January and March 1987 were already at an advanced stage of formulation before the Council Resolution of December 1986.

(b) However, there were areas where new action was undertaken as a *direct result* of policies proposed by the Resolution. An assessment of the Commission's response to the need for action to combat long-term unemployment appears, from the evidence of the follow-up report, to have been extremely positive. The Commission adopted a memorandum on combatting long-term unemployment 'in response to the request made in the Resolution' in May 1987. However, a memorandum issued by the Commission carries no status beyond that of a declaration of intent, and involves no commitment to action on the Commission's part.

The follow-up report further noted that the Commission was studying the development of the problem and assessing government measures to combat unemployment. The report outlined proposed Commission support for national campaigns, a study of the problems of measuring long-term unemployment, and the extension of Social Fund priority actions for the long-term unemployed to those aged under 25. Overall, with regard to long-term unemployment, the Commission's follow-up report depicted a situation in which clear initiatives had been taken within the framework laid down by the Council Resolution. More than any other area of the Action Programme for employment growth, Commission activity to combat long-term unemployment reflected a consensus between Commission and Council as to the policy required.

Only in the case of the Resolution call for an examination of the impact on the long-term

unemployed of social security systems within Member States, on which the Commission remained silent in the follow-up report, was there a lack of synergy between the Council and Commission on the objective of combatting long-term unemployment.

(iii) Where divergences occurred
A thorough assessment of those measures on which the follow-up report differed substantially from what was proposed in the Resolution is extremely difficult, due in part to the broad terms of reference used in the wording of both documents. Indeed, credit is perhaps due to those Commission officials who drafted the follow-up report for the extent to which those differences which did exist were minimised publically. Nevertheless, looking in particular at those areas where the Commission actively took decisions after December 1986 which were at odds with the aims and objectives of the Resolution, it is possible to discern instances where differences do occur.

For example, under heading 2: 'More efficient labour markets' the Resolution had called for (d) the removal of obstacles to the development of new forms of work on the periphery of traditional sectors of employment (this objective should be viewed in the context of draft directives, such as the proposed part-time work directive, which were under consideration at the time), in the sector of personal services and in activities which fulfil a public need, with the aim of meeting the changing requirements of society, and (e) the removal of obstacles to the development of part-time and temporary work, fixed term contracts and job sharing whilst preserving due regard for the need for social and employment protection. It can be assumed, with some degree of certainty, that what the UK Presidency had in mind in these particular areas was the achievement of progress towards greater labour market flexibility, in keeping with the themes of UK Government policy.

The follow-up report, making specific reference to points 2(d) and 2(e) of the Resolution on new forms of work, noted that the Commission was focussing its efforts 'chiefly at developing the Social Dialogue at Community level on the quantitative and qualitative adaptability of the labour market'.[7] Given the low priority afforded to the Social Dialogue in the Council Resolution, and the fact that the original UK draft did not include any reference to the role of the social partners, it can be assumed that Commission efforts to hold discussions with the two sides of industry on new forms of employment were not what was intended by the Council. Moreover, the clear differences between the policy intended by the Council and that being pursued by the Commission may indicate that the policy gulf was simply too great to be disguised on this particular point.

(iv) Where the Commission added greater emphasis
It is specifically with regard to the use of the social dialogue procedure that differences of emphasis between Council and Commission become clearly discernible.

Under heading 5 of the follow-up report: 'Social Dialogue', the Commission stressed progress achieved in the Social Dialogue process,[8] which was given equal weighting to the four priorities[9] highlighted in the Council Resolution (namely promoting new business and employment growth, creating more efficient labour markets, improving training and combatting long-term unemployment). The original draft of the Resolution contained no reference to the social partners, and the final text merely acknowledges the need to ensure more adaptable patterns of work *'in cooperation with the social partners'*,[10] acknowledges that Article 118B of the Treaty requires the Commission to endeavour to develop the dialogue between management and labour, and expresses the hope that the dialogue will continue.[11] It is therefore interesting to note the high profile of the Social Dialogue in the follow-up report.

Assessment of the follow-up report
The implication found in the follow-up report was that the Resolution on an Action Programme restated many of the objectives found in existing Community policy and did not require a change in emphasis for Commission activity. However, this is not altogether surprising given the rather uncontroversial aims of promoting new business and employment growth, encouraging more efficient labour markets, improving training, and combatting long-term unemployment which were laid down in the Resolution. It was certainly true that the Commission began to take initiatives in some of these areas long before the UK Presidency of 1986, and this was acknowledged in those parts of the Resolution which called for the rapid implementation of existing Community programmes.

With regard to new areas of activity proposed by the Resolution, we have already noted the generalised wording of some sections of the document. Furthermore, it may have been considered unusual to expect a Council Resolution on such a broad area of policy as employment growth to specify in precise detail what legislative proposals and administrative measures the Commission should make.

Commentators on the UK response to the Commission follow-up report have tended to stress the divergence between the Council Resolution and the results emanating from the Commission (see in particular Teague, 1989, and Brewster and Teague, 1989). Certainly there is some validity in these arguments to the extent that the UK objectives of labour market flexibility and deregulation are not the emphasis of the Commission's report. The fact is that given the framework within which the Commission operates and the emphasis of its report on specific policy initiatives, while the nominal divergence of the two documents may be narrow, the actual divergence between what the Resolution intended and what the Commission achieved may be rather broad.

In essence it is possible to see the Commission, while working within the framework laid down by the Resolution on an Action Programme on employment growth, utilising its central position in the policy-making process to interpret initiatives to achieve employment growth as a continuation of existing Community policy. It is, nevertheless, worth reiterating the point that in analysing Community policy it is often difficult to untangle what activities were *directly* prompted by the Council Resolution, since it must be interpreted within the complex environment of Community decision-making. The important point to make is that the Resolution for an Action Programme was not operating in isolation, but became integrated into the existing framework of Commission activity.

Report on social developments 1987
In the light of the relative importance given to the Action Programme on employment growth during the UK Presidency, it would have been anticipated that the Commission's annual Report on Social Developments the following year would have placed considerable emphasis on progress achieved by Commission activity in those areas specified in the Action Programme.

The Report, while noting the conclusions of the Standing Committee on Employment on 25 June which emphasised the importance of greater flexibility on the labour market and of the internal and external adaptation of firms in relation to employment, stated that:

> *'In this connection, the Commission forwarded a Communication[12] to the Council on the internal and external adaptation of firms in relation to employment, the main components of which were incorporated in the Council resolution of 22 December 1986[13] on an action programme for employment growth and in the resolutions on the restructuring of the labour market[14] adopted by the European Parliament*

in November 1986. The Communication stresses the fact that, at both national and Community level, there have been an increasing number of negotiations and agreements on the subject of adaptability and flexibility in the light of the principles outlined in the Cooperative Growth Strategy for More Employment' [emphasis added].

From this extract of the Report on Social Developments it is evident that the Commission was, a year after adoption of the Council Resolution on an Action Programme on employment growth, presenting the Council intiative as little more than a continuation of Commission-led initiatives on the adaptation of firms in relation to employment and on a cooperative growth strategy. This interpretation was at odds with the way the Resolution for an Action Programme had been presented by the Labour and Social Affairs Council in December 1986. The essence of the Anglo-Irish-Italian initiative was that due to the shortcomings of Commission policies to encourage employment growth, there was a need for the Council to take the initiative by presenting to the Commission a ready-made action programme, which the latter was requested to implement.

It was noted above that the first report on the Commission's follow-up to the Council Resolution on an Action Programme on employment growth was published on 10 November 1987, eleven months after adoption of the Resolution, despite the fact that the latter had called for a progress report every six months.

At the meeting of Directors-General for Employment and Directors of Employment Services on 26-27 April 1988, almost six months after the first follow-up report, the second report on the implementation of the 1986 Council Resolution was examined.[15] Despite the fact that the second report had clearly been prepared prior to this meeting, it was never published by the Commission, and not referred to again in official Community documentation.

Assessment of the UK 1986 Presidency

Diplomatic success
The adoption of the Resolution on an Action Programme on employment growth and the ability to gain agreement on the text proposed by the UK Government at the Social Affairs Council was initially considered a significant diplomatic success of the Presidency. Having recognised the common theme of the need to combat unemployment running through the Irish and Italian Presidencies of 1984-85, the UK

built an Anglo-Irish-Italian initiative around the need for a coordinated Community action programme for employment growth. It was this joint initiative, coupled with the fact that the UK held the Presidency of the Council, which gave the initiative the durability necessary to overcome the initial indifference of the Commission and the doubts of other member states as to the wisdom or likely practical success of the project.

Technical success
The Resolution on an Action Programme on employment growth was a short-term or 'technical' success for three reasons:

(i) In terms of domestic political consumption, the unanimous support of the Council for what was, in essence, a reiteration of UK domestic policy towards job creation, was seen to be desirable;

(ii) The Resolution was a genuine attempt to give the problem of unemployment in the Community a higher profile and to put employment issues on the agenda;

(iii) By way of making a political statement, the Action Programme was successful in showing that there was another approach to combatting unemployment. The Commission had previously stated that no alternative was available to its strategy of cooperative growth and strengthening the Social Dialogue process.[16] The UK-led initiative showed that a non-interventionist market based approach could offer a viable alternative. It also put on the agenda the idea that Community action should not add unnecessarily to costs at the expense of jobs - a theme the UK Government was to return to often during its opposition to various aspects of the Social Action Programme. Expressed in these terms, the very existence of the Resolution was an achievement for the UK Presidency.

Relations with the Commission
While the UK administration appears to have been most successful in its bi-lateral relations with other member states, and in its recognition of the importance of achieving a consensus in the Council, some commentators have suggested that there may have been an overall failure to appreciate the role of the Commission in the Community policy process (Welsh, 1988, pp. 19). Such a view, of course, would fail to recognise the central role the Commission plays within the EC in respect of policy formulation and monitoring. The UK Government did hold meetings with the Commission officials to discuss the Action Programme well before the Presidency, and received neither an enthusiastic nor a negative response from the Commission.

Despite the inherent difficulty in untangling the complex web of Commission activity, from the evidence found in the Commission's official response to the Resolution on an Action Programme on employment growth, we have observed a variety of Commission strategies for dealing with policy divergences.

Clearly, the Commission took the issues raised by the UK-led initiative very seriously. Employment and job creation were issues which could not be ignored. Despite serious misgivings, the Commission, and for that matter the ETUC, had to show an interest in such an important issue.

A measure of the importance which the Commission attached to the initiative can be seen by the fact that Jean Degimbe, Director-General of DG V, is reported to have attended every working group meeting on the initiative. This provides evidence to support the view that the Action Programme was from the beginning an issue on which the Commission showed the utmost interest. It is most probably also the case that the Commission saw the Resolution as a threat to its own activities in the field of job creation. This factor was reflected in its response in the first follow-up report.

There was no sustained attempt by member states to dislodge the Commission from its established position on preferred methods of achieving employment growth, namely through recourse to the cooperative growth strategy and initiatives taken on the basis of agreements reached through the Social Dialogue process. Indeed, it is highly unlikely that it would have been possible to do so. Attempting this level of influence on the Commission would have been unrealistic, particularly, as we noted above, due to the fact that the Commission has its own policy agenda and its own political dynamic. The task of arguing the UK position in a pre-emptive way by winning the support of Commission officials was never undertaken.

Concluding remarks

The Resolution highlighted concern on the unemployment problem. Yet follow-through activity was not undertaken for the reasons outlined above, namely the difficulty in influencing the Commission, which had its own priorities in the field of social policy, domestic concerns which took priority at the time, and the nature of the six month revolving Presidency process, which made it difficult to establish policy continuity at an intergovernmental level.

Footnotes on Section 3

1. Standing Committee on Employment Press Release 10305/86 (Presse 163), pp. 3 and pp. 6.

2. OJC 322, 15 December 1986, pp. 15.

3. European Parliament Minutes, 11 November 1986.

4. COM(87) 474 final.

5. OJC 340, 31 December 1986, pp. 6.

6. OJC 340, 340, 31 December 1986, pp. 3, para 10.

7. COM(87) 474 final, pp. 4.

8. COM(87) 474 final, pp. 10.

9. Promoting new business and employment growth, creating more efficient labour markets, improving training and combatting long-term unemployment.

10. OJC 340, 31 December 1986, pp. 3.

11. OJC 340, 31 December 1986, pp. 5.

12. COM(87) 229 final.

13. OJC 340, 31 December 1986.

14. OJC 322, 15 December 1986.

15. Bulletin of the European Communities, Vol. 21 No. 4 1988, pp. 32-33.

16. See in particular Council Decision 85/619/EEC of 20 December 1985 on acceptance of the annual economic report and laying down economic guidelines for 1986. OLJ 377, 31 December 1985.

Section 4
Implementing Policy

European Union legislation is designed to have particular outcomes on a specified policy area in each member state. Achieving these outcomes clearly requires EU law to be in a form capable of achieving these stated goals. Yet no matter how appropriate the design and form of a legislative instrument may be, objectives will not be met unless EU law is correctly transposed into national law, in the case of a Directive, and subsequently complied with by those whose behaviour the new law is intended to regulate or modify.

The impact of EU law thus becomes dependant upon prompt and accurate implementation by national governments. Assuming that transposition of EU law into national statute is achieved in an appropriate manner, the effective enforcement of these legal provisions in all parts of the Union then becomes the responsibility of national agencies whose duty it is to ensure compliance with the law.

In many instances, implementation of EU legislation into national law has been slow and practical enforcement even slower. As a result, although legislation may have been adopted at EU level some time ago, it may still fail to be effective (a point illustrated by a case study of the tachograph regulation: Butt Philip, 1988). The EU needs to address why this is the case and ensure either that legislation is implemented or, where this is not possible, repealed. This issue has become a common theme in the EU policy debate. The UK Government has consistently highlighted the importance of this issue. During the 1992 UK Presidency, for instance, it stressed that the full benefits of EU law on health and safety at work can only be achieved through even-handed implementation and enforcement of such legislation across the Union (Employment Department, 1993). In December 1993, one of the most telling arguments in the UK's contribution to the debate on Growth, Competitiveness and Employment (HM Treasury/Employment Department, 1993) was that the Union should be aware of the likely consequences of regulatory changes that it proposes. One of the reasons for poor implementation is that member states and important groups within them are put off once they realise the full costs implied.

An awareness of these consequences requires accurate compliance assessments ('fiches d'impact').

In terms of cost, it must be demonstrated that legislation is capable of fulfilling policy goals in the most efficient manner. The costs and benefits of regulation will be distorted unless regulations are implemented, enforced and complied with in all parts of the Union and the introduction of the legislation in those circumstances could result in a less integrated and more discriminatory European Union than before. Such assessments must also demonstrate the ability of legislation to achieve the benefits intended.

Yet despite a wide consensus that effective implementation, even-handed enforcement and appropriate levels of compliance must be ensured, no agreement has yet been reached on how this objective should be met. This section explores the detail of what is entailed by implementation, enforcement and compliance, explains the links between the three concepts, assesses the impact of regulatory enforcement and considers how improvements can be made to the principal mechanisms currently used to ensure the effectiveness of EU law at European Union level.

Implementation

In this context, implementation is the process giving effect at national level to EC law. By implementation of European law we mean that it is enacted into national statute and administrative practice: not only the way it is transposed into national law.

In assessing the effectiveness of current mechanisms to ensure the implementation of European Union law, particular attention must be focused on the implementation of EU law (directives) into national law (statute or administrative measures). The Council and Commission are both empowered to issue regulations which, once adopted, automatically become part of the national legal framework in each member state without the necessity for legislative or administrative implementation. Yet while regulations are directly applicable they do often require member states to take action to ensure compliance with their provisions, such as in the case of the tachograph Regulation of 1969. A directive adopted by the Council, on the other hand, requires member states to implement national laws, regulations and administrative provisions necessary to bring national legislation into line with EU law. In allowing member states to choose the exact form in which it is transposed into national law, directives offer member states discretion in the method of national implementation.

Once a directive has been adopted member states are normally given between 18 and 36 months to transpose it. Implementation has three components: the establishment of rights and obligations as laid down in the text of the directive, the amendment of contradictory national legislation and the creation of the necessary structures to ensure that the terms of the directive are carried out.

Once a directive has been transposed into national law it is assumed that an individual upon whom the directive has conferred rights will rely not on the directive, but on national implementing legislation. Through this procedure, the intention is that a directive will provide for national diversity and variation within the permitted scope of the directive's text. It is not expected that every member state will have identical legislation to achieve the same effect. Rather, as Freestone and Davidson (1988) have recognised, directives impose obligations of the result to be achieved by a choice of means, while Regulations impose obligations of form, in the sense that a Regulation automatically becomes an integral part of the national legal system.

The means by which member states implement EU directives into national law vary considerably according to legal traditions and the peculiarities of existing national procedures. Yet despite the diversity of national administrative frameworks, the policy outcome is intended to be the same.

Directives involve a two-phase legislative procedure according to which member states must agree the enactment of the text at EU level and then transpose the directive into national law. However, because directives in the field of social policy (which normally take as their legal basis Articles 118 or 118A, although other Articles are also used) are designed to harmonise minimum standards, particularly on health and safety, or allow for mutual recognition of differing national approaches to the law, the character of national transposing legislation may differ in each member state. The resulting problems for ensuring uniform effectiveness of EU law are well-known. A member state may fail to transpose a directive into national law at all, may do so only partially or inadequately. Even following transposition, the uniform application of EU law is dependent on the interpretation of national statutes in national courts. Although Article 177 of the EEC Treaty provides a mechanism for national courts to refer problems of interpretation of EU law to the European Court of Justice, the onus remains with a national court to seek clarification on a point of EU law from the European Court. The role of the European Court under the Article 177 preliminary ruling procedure thus

remains one of interpretation, not application of EU law. The effectiveness of EU law remains dependent on the quality and particular idiosyncrasies of national legal systems.

Meeting the deadline
One concern is that EU directives are not properly implemented into national law within the agreed timetable. By the end of 1992, while the United Kingdom had implemented 97 per cent of directives applicable to employment and social policy (more than any other member state), and Denmark and Ireland had implemented 91 per cent of these directives, seven other member states had implemented 70 per cent or less of the same legislation (Commission of the EC, 1993).

At the intergovernmental level, these concerns have been articulated by a 'Declaration on the Implementation of Community Law' attached to the Maastricht Treaty. This declaration enjoined member states to transpose directives fully and adequately into national law within the specified deadlines and stated that, while member states might take different measures to enforce EU law, these should result in the law being applied with the same effectiveness and rigour as national law. Is this commitment being met by the member states?

Empirical evidence published in 1986 distinguished between different types of non-compliance (Krislov et al, 1986). These included failure to implement and enforce European law into national law, failure to apply the law, and failure to enforce it (either at an administrative or a judicial level).

The Commission's own Sutherland Report (1992) acknowledged the problem of ensuring even-handed enforcement at the national level and a related report by Dehousse et al (1992) has put forward ideas about the new regulatory mechanisms which may be needed. To overcome the failure of some member states to adequately implement and enforce EU law, the Sutherland Report suggests the use of directly applicable regulations instead of directives (for which transposition is required) but also acknowledges that this would be difficult to accommodate in some national legal structures.

Gaining competitive advantage
These concerns reflect not only the complexity of EU law, but also the transformation of legal, economic and political life within western Europe since the 1950s. With withdrawal from the Community no longer an option for member states for a variety of economic and political reasons, some commentators (Weiler, 1991, for instance) have suggested that in

order to avoid the rigours of closer integration, member states are increasingly resorting to a new strategy of non-compliance - or, to be more accurate, selective compliance, with EU law through imprecise transposition into national law or through uneven enforcement of the law through national agencies. Inactive membership or selective enthusiasm for implementing (or enforcing) EU law not only becomes a viable alternative to withdrawal, but also allows a member state to maximise the benefits of gaining access to the domestic markets of others, while minimising the costs of actually complying with the legal requirements to do so. In other instances, non-compliance may be sought for domestic political reasons, such as the German threat to ban imports of British beef.

While there may be administrative reasons why member states delay implementing EU law, without deviating from the letter of the law, there may also be strong economic and political reasons why member states may wish to implement and enforce EU law in a particular manner which is advantageous to domestic actors. Variation in regulatory stringency may provide a source of competitive advantage.

Monitoring implementation
It is difficult to evaluate the extent of the problem accurately. Our knowledge of implementation of EU law by member states has recently been described as a 'black hole' (Weiler, 1991). Part of the problem stems from the availability and comparability of data. Other problems relate directly to non-compliance by member states.

Two particular issues are worthy of note. First, the general trend has been an increase in the number of instances in which member states fail to comply with a judgement of the Court of Justice. On 31st December 1992 the Commission's tenth annual report on the application of Community law (Commission of the EC, 1993) gave a cumulative figure of 90 Court judgments that had not been complied with. Second, there has been a failure by member states to transpose directives adequately at all representing an obstacle to the credibility of EU law as a whole (Anderson, 1988).

Ensuring implementation
Two EU institutions are commonly seen as having the tools and techniques capable of ensuring implementation of European Union law. First, variations in the interpretation of EU law when transposed into national law are monitored by the Commission and second, are enforced by the Court of Justice. The role of these institutions is discussed below. In addition, although no formal procedures exist for the Council or European Parliament to sanction member states for failure to implement EU law, political pressure from these bodies may become a key element in ensuring implementation.

Compliance

Once a directive has been passed into domestic legislation, the next step is to ensure compliance with its terms. Compliance refers to behaviour that conforms to a pre-determined set of regulatory measures. It implies not just avoiding breaking the law but acting in a manner envisaged by those who framed it. Compliance therefore amounts to reactive behaviour through which the targets of EU policy should be met. Maintaining high levels of compliance requires ongoing negotiation with those from whom compliant behaviour is sought, enforcement and organisational change in administrative agencies. Compliance is sought both for its own sake, to ensure that the intended benefits of regulation actually occur, and in order to remove competitive advantage from those who do not carry the cost of compliance. This is the 'level playing field' argument.

Achieving consistently high levels of compliance in all member states requires enforcement systems in each country to demonstrate an equal degree of effectiveness. A measure of the effectiveness of differing national systems of implementing and enforcing EU law must ultimately be the extent to which target groups (companies, for instance) respond to regulatory regimes in the way intended. It must also be acknowledged that different legal traditions result in the use of different methods for implementing and enforcing EU law with, for example, collective agreements playing a central role in some member states.

For companies, if effective compliance is to be achieved appropriate changes in behaviour are likely to be required. Yet the extent of the problem will vary if, in some member states existing national law will cover the point so no behavioural change is required. Furthermore, improved standards of enforcement by national agencies may not be sufficient to ensure full compliance with EU law. Broadly speaking there are three scenarios which best describe (company) responses to regulation and enforcement: full compliance, non-compliance and creative compliance.

Full compliance with EU law is likely to occur where there are limited or 'normal' levels of transgression from the rules and a general consensus on policy goals and the need for legislation, for example, where an employer is genuinely concerned about the welfare of employees. Work at NIESR, for instance, has shown that in general there is full compliance with redundancy provisions in Germany (Mayes and Soteri, 1994). This is both because the legal principles are widely accepted and because of the stringent nature of the regulations which make them extremely difficult to avoid. Full compliance may also indicate that the costs of compliance are not disproportionately high.

Where compliance costs outweigh the benefits, employers may react in one of two ways: either they may comply under duress because efficient enforcement mechanisms and large penalties make the threat of detection for non-compliance a sufficient deterrent, or they may opt not to comply, substantially deviating from the requirements of the law rather than non complying at all, and considering the likelihood of detection and sanctions sufficiently small to warrant the risks involved. The financial benefits of non-compliance, however, become difficult to quantify, in health and safety for instance, once one considers the effect of potential increases in insurance premiums resulting from accident claims or the loss of productivity while skilled workers are absent due to occupational sickness or injury.

Establishing an efficient enforcement regime and setting large fines for non- compliance may not, however, meet the regulatory goal of securing particular policy objectives. The paradox of compliance may actually be that, rather than achieving the desired outcome from the enforcement process, formal compliance avoids the costs of regulation by entirely legal means. This is creative compliance (McBarnet & Whelan, 1991).

Creative compliance, obeying the letter of the law but avoiding its spirit, complying with the form of the law without complying in substance, constitutes a pre-emptive strategy for avoiding regulatory enforcement by circumventing the law's objectives without breaking the rules (McBarnet & Whelan, 1992). This is a form of the 'unintended' consequences of regulation mentioned earlier.

There is some evidence, for example, of pre-emptive compliance with the Directive on the European Works Councils (EWCs). There are now twenty or more multi-national companies in Europe which have introduced their own arrangements for information disclosure and, more rarely, consultation. Research at NIESR indicates that there are a number of management rationales for recognising these bodies, including their usefulness in explaining company restructuring at European level to employees and

their value in pre-empting EU legislation. Since the terms of the EWCs Directive exempt companies with existing arrangements, such pre-emptive measures can be seen as a form of creative compliance, avoiding the impact of legislation by taking action early enough in the process. From the point of view of the company (the regulatee) this provides a means of avoiding the costs of compliance.

If national measures to implement EU law are used creatively by innovative actors to gain advantages over their competitors in the domestic market or elsewhere in the Union, regulation may actually open up new sources of advantage through entirely legal means.

Where creative compliance is occurring the law is being complied with, but in a manner which avoids its intended consequences. Instead the law itself becomes an instrument of creative compliance. Work at NIESR points to a measure of creative compliance to avoid generous redundancy provisions in the Netherlands (Mayes and Soteri, 1994). By taking on temporary rather than permanent staff, or by classifying workers as 'incapacitated' rather than 'redundant', costly payments may be avoided by legal means.

While evasion involves ignoring or breaking the law, avoiding regulation relies entirely on legal methods to neutralise its impact. Olsen (1992) describes how a company can avoid health and safety requirements by responding to improvement notices in a number of ways, including sending letters to the inspectorate explaining why they cannot solve the problem, calling high-profile meeting to discuss the problem or appointing consultants to undertake lengthy reviews. Each of these actions responds to the inspectorate's demands by reflecting on the problem without actually solving it. This type of approach attempts to convince an inspectorate that a company takes the enforcement process seriously and is seeking to rectify the breach of health and safety law. For the period that the inspectorate remains satisfied with the response, the company successfully avoids the financial costs of compliance - at least until the inspectorate next visits the factory.

Put another way, enforcement is only capable of ensuring compliance with legal form (the letter of the law). Ensuring compliance with legal substance (the spirit of the law) is a much more complex problem. Evasion of legal requirements (creative compliance) poses entirely different problems of avoidance. Where the law is being avoided, improved enforcement may ensure tolerable levels of compliance. Where the law is being evaded, enforcement is much more of a problem.

Detection is virtually impossible (although other agents with interests at stake, such as trade unions, lobby groups or other firms, may have a role to play in monitoring and enforcing compliance (McBarnet, 1992). Trade unions have a specific impact on how the law is enforced at workplace level. Walters and Freeman (1992) have described the role of formalised procedures for trade union participation in ensuring that employers comply with health and safety at work legislation. Lobby groups also have an important role to play in ensuring compliance with EU law. Environmental groups, for instance, influence the way that the law is applied by alerting the Commission to instances where there is a failure to implement EU law. Firms, on the other hand, will be motivated to ensure that others comply with legislation by a desire to prevent competitive distortions accruing to rival companies.

While creative compliance is particularly prevalent in accounting, its existence in the context of labour law may have particularly serious ramifications, for example on standards of health and safety in the workplace. In social policy areas the consequences of 'avoidance' are not, as with, say, taxation, only in terms of loss of government revenue but also in terms of loss of sickness, injury or loss of life. The moral incentives for employers to comply with both the spirit and the letter of the law are therefore particularly strong, as should be the motivation for national enforcement agencies to ensure that regulations are neither avoided or evaded, regardless of the competitive advantages which may accrue to a company from avoiding the cost of complying with national or EU law.

Enforcement

The possibility of non-compliance or creative compliance requires national authorities to monitor or police compliance with the legislation and bring those responsible for non-compliance into line.

Interactions between detailed EU directives and existing national legislative frameworks may lead to different policy outcomes in different parts of the Union. This is because the framework of law applied in each member state differs, sometimes in important respects. As a result, the effectiveness of national enforcement systems relative to one another becomes extremely difficult to assess. Both implementation and compliance may be dependent on enforcement mechanisms such as incentives, recourse to legal sanctions, or the imposition of financial sanctions. Effective enforcement will be only achieved once target groups comply with legislation in the way intended. Compliance should be achieved by effective enforcement.

Levels of enforcement
The enforcement of EU law occurs on a number of levels: (i) infringement proceedings brought by the Commission and enforced by the European Court against member states for failure to implement EU law; (ii) monitoring compliance with, and ensuring the enforcement of, nationally-implemented EU law by national enforcement agencies, for example the enforcement of health and safety at work law by the Health and Safety Executive in Great Britain; (iii) the enforcement of EU law by individuals through litigation in a national court, for example enforcing rights emanating from a directive which has direct effect, such as the right to equal treatment.

The fact that EU legislation has by nature already been agreed upon by member states means that the issue is one of enforcing agreed policy goals, ensuring compliance with agreed standards and bringing those responsible for non-compliance into line.

EU legislation, however, is also the result of negotiation and compromise between EU institutions, national governments and agreed by the Council of Ministers. This may be a source of divergence as well as consensus. Siedentopf and Hauschild (1988) have described how, in Roman law countries where prescriptive legislation is the norm, the prevailing view is that where negotiation results in compromise at the lowest level, the quality of regulation may be undermined. The ability of member states to enforce common standards which are set out in imprecise, general regulations may therefore be seriously impaired. The UK has advocated goal-setting legislation to address this problem.

Unless the objectives to be met are sufficiently clear, and unless a measure is then effectively implemented and enforced in all parts of the Union, competitive distortions will result, ensuring that the costs and benefits of regulation are not evenly distributed.

Common standards may be formalistic measures (the command and control approach), strictly enforced by the State and offering little leeway for variations in response, or more general measures to which a wider range of acceptable responses may be given.

Enforcement by EU institutions

The Commission obtains cases either pro-actively through its own investigations or reactively in the form of complaints. On average about 85 per cent of complaints are from companies, 5 per cent from private individuals, 5 per cent from the European Parliament and 5 per cent from member states (Snyder, 1993). Under Article 169 the Commission enters into two formal stages for infringement proceedings: (i) an administrative stage in which the Commission invites a member state to submit observations on the alleged breach and delivery by the Commission of a reasoned opinion, (ii) a judicial stage in which the Commission brings the matter before the European Court.

Using judgments of the European Court and the national courts to ensure the effective implementation of EU law has several disadvantages which flow from the way that the system has evolved. Foremost among these is that, by definition, judicial rules have been developed in an ad hoc way, less coherent and less comprehensive than a legislative framework. Litigation rates are influenced by diverse legal cultures and differ substantially among member states. This alone would make it unlikely that individual litigation would result in the uniform effectiveness of EU law.

Snyder (1990) has suggested that this lack of coherence may be so great that it might be appropriate to enact legislation to harmonise selected elements of national systems of remedies for the enforcement of EU rights such as time limits and the availability of interim relief. Otherwise member states may fail adequately to fulfil their obligations under Article 5 and individuals may find EU law to be ineffective.

The next section explores some of these enforcement issues in the context of EU legislation on health and safety at work, with the focus on the UK unitary system of enforcement, the German federal system, the French codified system and the Italian system which, judged on the terms of the Italian Senate's own Parliamentary Inquiry, has been malfunctioning.

Enforcing EU health and safety law in the UK, Germany, France and Italy

There are several reasons for choosing health and safety at work for particular attention. It is one of the most well-established areas of EU social policy, with initial legislation dating back to the early 1960s (James, 1993). As a result there is a corpus of legislation there to analyse. In addition, it is one of the few areas of labour market policy in which there is a consensus supporting regulation in all member states. It is also an extremely important area of policy for employers and employees alike - everyone has an interest in improving standards.

Matthews (1993) outlines the main powers of HSE and local authority inspectors in Great Britain, Gewerbeaufsichtsämte (GAs) and Berufsgenoßenschaften (BGs) in Germany, the Labour Inspectorate and Caisses Regionales d'Assurance Maladie (CRAMs) in France, and inspectors of the local health units in Italy. This indicates that, although each national system has the same objective of ensuring effective and even-handed enforcement of health and safety law, a considerable variation in enforcement techniques can be identified.

Organisation of inspectorates

Enforcement of EU law on health and safety at work involves both top-down and bottom-up approaches to interpretation of the rules, the former involving highly centralised control, the latter involving local administration.

Great Britain operates what is essentially a unified system in that one inspection authority covers all health and safety rules for each firm, with inspectors from the Field Operations Division working under the co-ordination of the Health and Safety Executive for some firms and local authority inspectors for others. This differs from the situation in Germany where a dual system of enforcement is in operation, within which the Gewerbeaufsichtsämte (GAs) and Berufsgenoßenschaften (BGs) perform complementary functions which are fundamental to the operation of the system. In France, as in Germany, insurance inspectors play an important role in the enforcement process. Insurance inspectorates in Germany and France do, however, have more limited powers than their counterparts from labour inspectorates with regard to enforcement. Italy operates a system which is highly decentralised, with little central control in terms of co-ordination retained by the Ministry of Health. This is perhaps a contributory factor to the uneven levels of compliance with health and safety legislation in Italy.

Scope of responsibilities

Health and safety enforcement is the primary function of the inspectorates in all four member states. Outside this core activity, however, differences do exist in the scope and range of areas for which each inspectorate carries responsibility. In Great Britain, the responsiblities of the HSE include ensuring the health and safety of the public affected by work activities, while in other member states responsibility for public safety lies with the police. In Germany, the duties of the GAs include not only health and safety, but also monitoring compliance with environmental standards in the workplace.

Unlike the Health and Safety Executive in Great Britain, most Land GAs also have responsibility for enforcing environmental protection measures, such as by giving permission for construction projects or monitoring emission controls. While it remains difficult to ascertain the exact amount of time allocated to each responsibility, the HSE have estimated that environmental protection tasks occupy half of GA inspectors' time (HSE, 1991), although this varies between Länder.

As part of our own research, we spoke to a number of GAs to ascertain the amount of inspectors' time spent on each area of responsibility. Bremen, for instance, allocates between 20 and 30 per cent of time to monitoring emission levels, with the remaining time spent on various aspects of work protection, including health and safety. In Schleswig-Holstein the figure is higher, with the GA devoting 42 per cent of inspectors' time to monitoring emission levels and other environmental issues. In Lower Saxony (Niedersachsen) the situation is different again: while in the past up to 30 per cent of inspectors' time was spent on monitoring emission levels, the allocation of time was altered in 1993, with 50 per cent of time spent on monitoring emissions and the remaining 50 per cent on enforcing work protection legislation.

Obviously the amount of time spent on monitoring emission levels reduces time available for other tasks. In the former DDR Länder responsibility for enforcing environmental protection lies not with the GAs but with the Land Environment Ministries, where the implication is that the efforts of GA inspectors are deliberately being concentrated on improving health and safety standards in the new eastern regions of Germany.

The amount of time available for monitoring and enforcing health and safety at work legislation in Germany is further influenced by the fact that GAs are also responsible for other aspects of labour protection, such as maternity rights and the protection of young workers. The HSE (1991) estimate that the amount of time available for monitoring and enforcing health and safety measures amounts to only 10 to 15 per cent of time for the GAs. In response to our own investigations on this point, the Schleswig-Holstein GA provided a higher figure of 38 per cent of time spent on technical aspects of work protection. This estimate may, however, be

misleading since 'work protection' of a technical nature includes, in addition to health and safety at work, other aspects of the Arbeitsstattenverordnung, such as giving permission for new construction projects. Variation in policy responsibility thus constitutes an important reason for enforcement fragmentation.

There is no national policy on where and when inspection visits should be made in Germany. The decision on where efforts should be concentrated is left to the GA in each Land. Figures quoted in the Arbeitssicherheit for 1991, for instance, show that in Lander of comparable size and structure, such as Lower Saxony (Neidersachsen) and Bavaria (Bayern) different levels of enforcement action were taking place between 1988 and 1990.

There may be a number of reasons for the differences in these figures: (i) standards of health and safety may be generally better in one Land than another; (ii) the policies adopted by the various enforcement agencies may differ, for example, on the extent to which informal advice is given prior to formal enforcement procedures; (iii) attitudes of the courts towards prosecutions for health and safety offences differ; (iv) the enforcement agencies alter emphasis of their monitoring and enforcement activities, focusing on different fields of their work from time to time.

Following the line of argument in (iv), we spoke to a number of Land GAs to ascertain their policy on targeting specific issues for their monitoring and enforcement work. Bremen, for example, replied that while they were able to monitor all aspects of health and safety in a small company, in medium and large sized companies this is not possible. Inspectors instead target certain areas of health and safety, or particular parts of the company.

The Bremen GA undertake special monitoring campaigns which focus on specific aspects of health and safety, such as construction site noise, with the objective of ensuring that all workers exposed to high noise levels wear adequate protection. Special campaigns in Bremen last up to two weeks and occur between two and four times a year.

In Schleswig-Holstein special monitoring campaigns tend to be in areas where recent accidents have occurred. If, for example, a serious accident has occurred on a particular machine, inspectors will check the safety of all similar equipment in other companies. Monitoring campaigns in 1992 included wood processing plants and chemical cleaning companies.

In Thüringen, a Land in the former DDR, special campaigns have reflected concern over the low safety standards in that region. Campaigns in 1992 included monitoring the safety of petrol stations and the compliance of employers with youth protection legislation.

In addition to the decentralised inspection framework, the role of insurance companies is an important factor which influences the character of national enforcement systems. In Germany all employers must be members of insurance schemes which provide compensation for employees injured at work. These schemes are funded by employers and administered by the Berufsgenoßenschaften (Employers' Associations for Accident Insurance). Membership of the Berufsgenoßenschaften (BGs) is compulsory, with different BGs for different types of companies.

Each BG organises inspections and issues additional accident prevention regulations (generally relating to technical standards of machinery or equipment) and monitor compliance with its own safety criteria. Its representatives ultimately have a direct bearing on the premium which an employer has to pay to the insurance association since contributions vary according to the safety rating of the undertaking. Financial considerations are thus a powerful incentive for employers to comply with BG regulations.

Enforcing health and safety law in France
There is also a division of enforcement responsibilities in France. The Labour Inspectorate enforce all parts of the Labour Code, while insurance funds (Caisses Regionales d'Assurance Maladie, or CRAMs) employ inspectors to make a broad assessment of health and safety standards in a workplace, estimating premiums on the basis of risk and the number of accidents recorded.

Both the French Labour Inspectorate and the CRAMs are organised along regional rather than sectoral lines, but like Germany share the absence of the unitary system of enforcement found in the UK. In France, duties of the Labour Inspectorate involve both health and safety enforcement, and conciliation in workplace industrial relations disputes.

Styles of enforcement
Differences in the organisation of enforcement activity are not, however, primarily the result of differing statutory arrangements. Our analysis of national legislative provisions in each member state has shown that similar regulatory arrangements exist in each of the four countries. Rather differences in

enforcement activity stem from variations in styles of enforcement, which Vogel (1986) has attributed to the national setting. On the basis of Vogel's analysis, one would expect the way in which EU law on health and safety at work is enforced in each member state to vary from that of other countries for reasons relating to the organisation of enforcement bodies and the style of enforcement activity adopted in that national setting. Amongst national health and safety inspectorates, styles of enforcement vary. Two principal styles of enforcement can be identified. Regulatory enforcement involves both legal action (the 'coercive approach') and informal modes of advice and persuasion ('the advisory approach').

To continue with the example of health and safety, national inspectorates possess a number of statutory powers which may be used to sanction companies or individuals for behaviour which does not conform with regulatory requirements. These sanctions may include referring cases for prosecution, issuing summary fines or closing a workplace.

The coercive model is therefore characterised by an emphasis on the rigorous application of rules, together with an enforcement style which is formal and follows the letter of the law.

Relying on legal procedures to achieve compliance, the coercive model has also been described as the 'sanctioning strategy' (Hawkins, 1984). Hutter (1989) even suggests that the number of prosecutions may in some instances be regarded by an inspectorate as a measure of policy success.

With the emphasis on providing information on how compliance with regulatory requirements can be achieved, legal sanctions are used only where there is a high risk of accidents or where the provision of advice does not achieve the desired outcome of ensuring compliance.

The advisory approach to enforcement may be sub-divided further by making the distinction between the persuasive approach and the insistent approach. Hutter (1989) characterises the persuasive approach as a situation where an inspector explains legal requirements and discusses with an employer how improvements can be best achieved. An employer is then given the opportunity to rectify problems without the threat of prosecution being imminent.

The insistent approach, on the other hand, relies on an inspector setting out the improvements to be made by an employer within a clearly defined time-scale, insisting on the ends to be achieved more often than insisting on the means of achieving those ends.

Where improvements are not made, the coercive approach will be brought into play relatively early in the process in order to ensure compliance. Hutter's field work with the UK factory inspectorate (Hutter, 1989), for example, enabled her to classify the UK approach as being closer to the insistent than the persuasive approach to enforcement.

The coercive and advisory models in perspective
In the context of health and safety at work, the two broad enforcement styles we have characterised are both relevant. Health and safety inspectors enforce regulatory requirements either by coercion (for example, orders, fines, prosecutions) or by providing advice which, in itself, ensures compliance with the law by encouraging an employer voluntarily to alter his behaviour. The incentive for employers to comply with EU law is dependent on a number of factors, including:

(i)   the frequency of inspections;

(ii)   the provision of advice on health and safety improvements;

(iii) warnings issued by inspectors;

(iv)   the imposition of higher insurance premiums (in Germany and France) for failure to comply;

(v)   the imposition of fines;

(vi)   temporary closure of premises;

(vii) prosecution through the courts.

A measure of the effectiveness of each national approach towards enforcement must ultimately be measured by the extent to which companies respond to the regulatory regimes in which they operate. Based on a primarily economic argument, an explanation of the reasons why companies comply with the law would emphasise the threat of sanctions imposed for non-compliance. If the cost of fines is smaller than the financial benefits of not complying, the motivation to avoid regulation will be great - the benefits of non-compliance outweighing the costs of compliance.

It is difficult, however, to understand why companies comply with advice given by health and safety inspectors simply by reference to financial motives. Although there must be an element of avoiding sanctions imposed for non-compliance, it seems likely that there are also other reasons why employers comply with health and safety regulations. One reason might be that they are interested in the welfare of employees. Another may be that it is actually more efficient to follow legal guidelines when carrying out their commercial activities.

Our analysis of the enforcement procedures in four member states supports the view that the advisory and coercive modes are both used, often in a complimentary fashion, with each regime seeking to utilise particular enforcement styles in preference to others.

As a general rule, the enforcement style most often favoured by health and safety inspectors in the four countries examined is the advisory approach. This model of enforcement accords closely with that recognised by Richardson, Ogus & Burrows (1983) and Hutter (1989), who referred to the 'accommodative' model of enforcement, characterised by the co-operative , conciliatory approach of enforcement officers, who seek to achieve compliance through persuasion, negotiation and education.

Labour inspection is moving towards a more advisory style of enforcement. Campbell (1986) attributes this increased role of advice to the growth of self-regulation by employers and worker representatives. This trend stems from the underlying philosophy that inspectors act in a conciliatory manner, except in serious cases. In some member states, the move away from strict enforcement has been accompanied by the introduction of general framework regulations, replacing overly prescriptive measures.

The advisory approach should not, however, be seen as an alternative to the coercive approach. Where companies seek not to comply with the law, either because of the high cost of compliance, or because they do not anticipate that the threat of prosecution is real, the coercive approach must be available to ensure even-handed and effective enforcement of EU law on health and safety at work. Above all, the threat of sanctions must be real and be used where appropriate.

Assessing the costs of compliance

The importance of compliance cost-benefit assessments
Comprehensive cost assessments (CCAs) have the potential to significantly enhance the quality of European Union law, demonstrating that legislation is capable of meeting the purpose for which it is intended and fulfilling policy goals in the most efficient manner. Cost benefit assessments (CBAs), on the other hand, show that a regulation is capable of meeting the goals for which it is intended also enhances the potential for gaining broad-based support for the implementation and enforcement of a policy measure across the Union.

The impact on small firms

There is a general presumption that cost/benefit analysis will result in regulation which is less burdensome on employers than if impact studies had not been undertaken. Research in the United States, for instance, has shown that small businesses do bear a disproportionate burden of the costs of regulation (Cole & Tegeler, 1980) since large companies are better equipped to spread compliance costs over a wider base. The Commission has already taken steps to assess the impact of regulations on small business via the fiches d'impact initiative. This is all to the good, but the likelihood is that it will fall short of the sort of study that would be necessary if a clear view of the trade-off that has to be made among the policy objectives is to be obtained. In preparing its impact studies, the Commission should be encouraged to be sufficiently analytical in assessing the impact of regulation in terms of costs and benefits, taking into account both long- and short-term considerations. Analysis of the regulatory impact on small firms should furthermore take place early in the drafting process so as to make an informed contribution to policy formulation.

Identifying reliable data sources

Since assumptions have the capacity to influence outcomes, access to sufficiently reliable information on the costs and benefits of regulation is essential. Uncertainties resulting from scarcity of reliable data, however, mean that accurate predictions about the impact of regulation are extremely difficult to make.

Resource limitations may make it necessary for the Commission to base estimates of regulatory costs and benefits on evidence derived from representative groups affected by the measure. In undertaking this task the Commission is likely to assess the degree of efficiency with which a regulation has achieved policy goals in their widest context, not just the impact on labour market efficiency and industrial competitiveness. Co-operation between Commission services, national governments and other interested parties (employers, employees and consumer groups) in the cost/benefit analysis process will be an essential part of this process.

If analysis relies on consultation between Commission services and representatives of employers and employees it is natural that each party will cast its submissions in a favourable light which reflects its view of the world (Breyer, 1979; McGarity, 1991). Overestimates of compliance costs may be given by employers, while employee representatives may exaggerate the benefits of regulation. Overestimation of costs and benefits will be inherent

in the process of analysis and impartial information will remain hard to come by.

Compliance cost assessment can usefully indicate the appropriateness of a particular regulatory approach, provided sufficient information about data sources and analytical techniques are made publicly available early in the policy process. While some bias can be removed by collecting impact assessments from various sources, ideally employer/employee estimates of costs and benefits will receive careful consideration and be subject to verification by independent agencies or with the aid of non-partisan data sources. Where information gaps are identified, or where it is necessary for cost/benefit analysis to make assumptions based on the predictions of interested parties, impact assessments must make clear the methodology used and data problems encountered. Where uncertainties remain, these must be acknowledged and taken into account.

Retrospective cost/benefit analysis studies

It is particularly important that some early testing of the effect of measures be undertaken because those which are intended to change behaviour will be poorly forecast as models are based on previous experience. For example job splitting has not been particularly common in the UK. Reductions in hours worked rather than reductions in the size of the labour force have tended to slow down structural change and by increasing costs reduce the capacity of firms in difficulty to invest.

It is a matter of concern that retrospective cost/benefit studies are not often attempted. Where retrospective economic impact studies have been undertaken, there are indications of a general trend towards overestimating compliance costs (Connerton & MacCarthy, 1982). Retrospective analysis of previous impact studies (namely those in the fiches d'impact) should be undertaken. This will fulfil an important function in the 'learning process' of assessing the regulatory costs and benefits if the role of impact assessments is to gain momentum in the European context.

Maximising the benefits, minimising the costs

Predicting the outcome of legislation is notoriously difficult. It must be acknowledged that policy decisions are often taken on the basis that certain approaches are intuitively correct, rather than on any notion of rational choice.

While there is a tendency to focus on regulatory costs, additional research into benefits is equally important. Analysing benefits helps clarify likely policy outcomes of legislation and may result in an acknowledgement that less (or more appropriate) measures are capable of achieving the same outcomes. Attention must also be paid to the benefits of legislation. Legislation on health and safety at work, for example, may result in lower accident and disease rates, in turn leading to less absenteeism by employees and reducing the cost of sick pay, administration costs, the need for temporary replacement workers and the likelihood of lower productivity levels. The HSE (1994) have estimated the cost of absence through injury for employers to be £400-£545 million per year in Great Britain.

Such benefits should receive due consideration in impact assessments. In other respects, the benefits of legislation are bound up in notions such as fairness and justice, concepts often considered immune to quantitative analysis (McGarity, 1991). Political goals will continue to inform policy outcomes as much as studies on costs and benefits. The role of the former in determining the outcomes of legislation at the European level should not be ignored.

Optimisation of benefits and costs will not always be an overriding priority and it is often a matter of secondary importance that the benefits of legislation can be shown to exceed the costs. Once a political and administrative solution to a perceived problem has been found, the Commission may be resistant to considering different alternatives to achieve the same objectives on grounds that it cannot afford to spend a great deal of time studying the long-range implications of its activities.

The Commission's aim will be to propose legislation which has a reasonable chance of adoption in the Council and which is capable of achieving a broad level of success in reaching the desired policy outcome.

Preference for a particular outcome very early in the process is, however, not consistent with rational cost/benefit analysis and would require the consideration of a range of options capable of achieving the same policy outcomes. While providing viable alternatives should play a key role in the policy process, in practice there will always be limitations on resources which will limit the capacity to examine a large number of policy options.

A statement on alternative legislative or non-legislative approaches which could achieve the same results, together with an indication of why such alternatives are not suitable and have not been chosen, should nevertheless be included in the analyses of proposed legislation.

What is required is for the European Commission to adopt an integrated approach, using cost/benefit analysis as a valuable tool in the policy process rather than a bureaucratic hurdle to be overcome. Studies should not be prepared after the fact as post hoc justification for policy decisions already reached on other grounds, but must be an integrated part of the design of legislation.

Systematically preparing cost/benefit analyses for even a few selected proposals requires substantial resources. Nevertheless, give the potential for cost/benefit analysis to improve the Community policy-process, carrying out accurate impact studies is an important task which the Commission should undertake at an early stage of the policy process for measures likely to involve significant compliance costs.

The monitoring process must generate data capable of enabling a systematic evaluation to be carried out. This requirement includes knowing what the position was before legislation was introduced and an ability to take into account other factors which might cause change during the observation period.

Cost-benefit analysis is well-known for being very inexact, greatly affected by assumptions and hence rather contentious. This is not a reason for not doing it, but a clear requirement to undertake analysis carefully and transparently. The UK has a long tradition of undertaking such studies and is in a good position to offer advice about how they should be done. This should not be on the basis that the UK approach is intuitively the correct one, but on the basis that the Union should follow 'best practice'.

Solving the problem of uneven compliance levels

A number of possible options exist which may enhance the potential for effective implementation, enforcement and compliance of EU law.

Harmonising statistics?
One obvious way to assess whether EU law is being adequately enforced and properly complied with would be to analyse statistical information on the outcomes that legislation is intended to influence and to draw conclusions from a comparison of data published by each member state. One policy area that would appear to lend itself to such analysis is health and safety at work. EU law on the protection of health and safety at work is a well-established area of EU legislative activity, with long traditions of

enforcement and national statistics compiled in broadly similar categories in all member states. Each member state, for instance, publishes information on the number of employers prosecuted for failure to comply with health and safety law. Each member state also publishes data on the incidence of accidents in the workplace, together with information on the number of fatalities which occur, and so on.

Since the primary objective of EU health and safety legislation is to prevent accidents at work and prosecute for the breach of common guidelines, one would expect analysis of different accident and enforcement rates to inform our understanding of the effectiveness of enforcement mechanisms in each member state. Under this simplified model, countries with high enforcement rates and a low incidence of accidents and injuries could then be viewed as 'good' enforcers of the law.

In practice, however, the incompatibility of statistics largely precludes such analysis. This incompatibility arises because even the way in which accident statistics are compiled in different member states varies enormously, to the extent that definitions of concepts as basic as an 'occupational fatality' have a number of different meanings in national data.

Each country publishes national statistics on industrial accidents and occupational diseases but, despite some attempts to present cross-national statistical information in a common form (OECD, 1989), this has so far only been done on the basis of collating existing national data. Large differences in the scope and categorisation of occupational accident statistics remain.

The data available reveal that a lack of standardisation in reporting requirements and in the classification of accidents and industrial activities will hinder the extent to which statistical comparison of occupational accident and illness rates can provide the necessary information to measure the effectiveness of national regulation and enforcement of health and safety at work provisions across member states.

The collection of statistics which are sufficiently similar would clearly be a step in the right direction towards making meaningful comparisons about the effectiveness of health and safety regulation and enforcement in each member state.

Initial steps towards standardising the information on EU accident statistics were taken by Eurostat in 1992. The publication of a paper on a 'Methodology for the harmonisation of European Occupational Accident Statistics' recommended the establishment of common variables and classification criteria on elements such as length of absence from work, reporting requirements, categories of workers excluded from statistics, classification of an 'industrial injury' and an 'occupational fatality'.

Our work on occupational accident statistics indicates the extent of problems likely to be encountered in assessing the impact of EU social policy in other areas. Our research found that, even in an area like health and safety where enforcement regimes are broadly similar and statistics are available in all member states, comparable data is extremely difficult to obtain. In other areas of EU social policy, where the quality of recorded information varies considerably, assessing the effectiveness of enforcement through statistical analysis becomes even more problematic.

Harmonising selected elements of national systems of remedies?
Some commentators (see in particular Snyder, 1993) have suggested that a greater degree of coherence may be achieved by partial harmonisation of national judicial remedies, such as time limits and the availability of interim relief. Proposals for this type of institutional harmonisation would, however, be unlikely to attract much enthusiasm from the member states themselves.

Creating new agencies?
Although the Commission has repeatedly stated its intention to go beyond implementation and systematically monitor the effectiveness with which national enforcement agencies apply EU law, Dehousse et al (1992) have expressed some doubts that it is well equipped to do so. They suggest that what may actually be required are EU level enforcement agencies. Through monitoring and issuing reports on the national enforcement regimes, some pressure may be imposed on member states which to not rigorously enforce the law to take a firmer line.

Yet given our earlier discussion of creative compliance, focusing on the enforcement of 'hard law' may not be capable of solving the whole problem. EU level agencies such as the European Agency for Health and Safety at Work have a role in the collection and dissemination of information throughout the EU, but the Agency does not have as its remit enforcement activities. European level enforcement agencies would, in any case, not solve the problem of compliance.

Encouraging self-regulation?
One possible way of pursuing a more flexible approach to enforcement - one capable of overcoming some of the problems of detection and creative compliance - may be for an enhanced role of self-regulation. The Standing Committee of Labour Inspectors, which comprises senior inspectors from all member states, deals with concerns over consistent implementation and enforcement through peer review. Particularly in cultures where there is a strong tradition of codes of conduct, 'gentlemen's agreements' and unwritten conventions, this may be a viable alternative to State intervention. Self-regulation, however, will only work effectively in member states where it has historically played a role. The principle of subsidiarity must determine how and where self-regulation is an appropriate mechanism. Pressures on the effectiveness of self-regulation may, however, intensify as a result of increased competition.

Reforming EU institutions?
The increasing penetration of EU and national administrative frameworks has created a new institutional environment. But because ensuring the effectiveness of EU law involves basic questions concerning the legitimacy of the Union and its scope for increased co-ordinating and monitoring powers, any consideration of how to improve the effectiveness of EU law leads to a wider debate on the role of EU institutions and the potential for their future development.

We have already noted that the institutional roles of the Commission (conducting administrative negotiation) and the Court of Justice (developing a judicial liability system) are crucial. Administrative negotiation and improved adjudication are not alternatives - within current levels of EU competence they should be developed in tandem to ensure that, at the national level, governments are doing sufficient to implement and enforce EU law. Ensuring the efficiency of current structures may be preferable to wholesale reform.

Creating new legislative instruments?
The question of whether the directive should be replaced by a EU act received serious consideration at the 1991 Intergovernmental Conference on Political Union. The proposal for a new 'EU law', directly applicable under the co-decision procedure and not requiring transposition into national law was, however, eventually eliminated from the Dutch Presidency's second draft of the Treaty. Instead, Declaration 16 was annexed to the Maastricht Treaty. This simply embodied an agreement that the 1996 Intergovernmental Conference will examine the extent to which it might be possible to review the classification of EU acts with a view to establishing an appropriate hierarchy between the different categories of act. The 1996 IGC will be an opportunity for agreed change in the EU legislative framework. In the meantime, the directive remains the most commonly used type of EU instrument. Any move towards more directly applicable EU law would, furthermore, raise issues of subsidiarity which, as defined in Article 3b of the Maastricht Treaty, presumes a preference for decentralisation where it may help ensure that government decisions adequately reflect local preferences.

Conclusions

Interactions between detailed EU directives and existing national legislative frameworks may lead to different policy outcomes in different parts of the Union. Furthermore, compliance with EU legislation may be indistinguishable from that of domestic leglislation, so actual levels of compliance with specific measures become extremely difficult to assess. Nevertheless, consideration should be given to whether a number of mechanisms and instruments are capable of ensuring the increased effectiveness of EU law.

What is actually required?
In ensuring the effectiveness of EU law, the current system has worked best where it has created legal principles and dealt with national administrations. Through adjudication and negotiation, EU-member state relations have been elaborated. However, neither the Commission nor the Court of Justice are sufficient to ensure the effectiveness of EU law without the co-operation and the commitment of government agencies, companies and individuals at the national level. To achieve this, new strategies, processes, tools and techniques may also be required.

These should include:

(i) EU law which is sufficiently clear and precise about the objectives to be met but, in accordance with the principle of subsidiarity, in a form which is not excessively prescriptive about the means to achieve it. The directive is likely to be the most appropriate instrument to fulfil this objective. In any case, making best use of existing legislative instruments will have more immediate impact than focusing on the need for new directly applicable forms of EU law.

(ii) Better co-operation between national enforcement agencies is sought through the Standing Committee of Labour Inspectors. Such mechanisms to exchange information and co-operation must be encouraged. They are an important step in establishing 'best practice' for national enforcement.

(iii) The collection of more information in the form of harmonised statistics is required before we can make informed value judgments about the effectiveness of each national implementation and enforcement system. How many infringements of EU law are taking place in each member state? How many prosecutions are occurring? This type of information is not available in a harmonised form.

This section has reviewed some of the problems involved in monitoring effective implementation, enforcement and compliance of EU law. It has focused on some of the issues involved in enforcing such legislation evenly as required to ensure both common standards and fair competition.

It is clear that we must avoid generalisations about the application of EU law. It is impossible, for instance, to substantiate the view that one country is 'more effective' in enforcing legislation than another.

What we can say, however, is that following a period of intense legislative activity since 1989, EU social policy should now enter a period of consolidation. Commission efforts must focus more sharply on the often neglected problems of ensuring effective implementation and enforcement of EU law if the costs and benefits of compliance are to be evenly distributed across all parts of the Union. Legislation should be reviewed and repealed where it is shown to be unnecessary, ineffective or damaging. Effective enforcement and compliance costs assessments are both areas where the UK has considerable experience and expertise. That expertise can fulfil an important role in informing the future EU social policy debate.

Section 5
Conclusions

This report has set out the findings of research conducted by the National Institute of Economic and Social Research on behalf of the Employment Department during the course of a three-year project over the period 1991 to 1994. This concluding section summarises the main findings of that research project.

Section 1 of the report provided an overview of the development of EC social and labour policy. It characterised the relationship between the European Commission and the member states as being fraught throughout the history of the European Communities because DG V of the Commission has interpreted its responsibilities in a broadly interventionist sense, seeking to ensure basic social and labour rights across all member states through legislation. Since the late 1980s, however, a less interventionist approach to these issues has become more widespread within the Commission (Commission of the EC, 1994a). By contrast, member states have always shown concern over what has sometimes been perceived to be an erosion of their powers by the Commission.

Section 2 examined the process by which EC social policy is formulated in practice, looking at the role of the various actors in that process. EC social policy formulation is characterised by informality and fluidity at the early stages. That informality and fluidity is largely due to the very nature of the Commission's responsibilities within the framework of the EC. It is required to draw up instruments which are supranational in character yet reflect the diversity of practice, traditions and legislation in fifteen member states. In order to achieve this task the Commission has adopted an 'open-door' approach by consulting widely. Such an approach concerns member states, especially when national perspectives diverge from the stance of the Commission. The UK government has fully appreciated that once the Commission has released the text of a draft instrument, its contents becomes much more difficult to influence. The UK government has successfully lobbied for the involvement of member states at an earlier stage in the formulation of policy, as well as for assessments of the likely costs of implementing proposed legislation.

Section 3 analysed the constraints on the formulation of policy through the Council. Using a case study of the Presidency, the section highlighted the difficulty of influencing the Commission when it has its own social policy priorities, and the constraints inherent in the Presidency process due to the six month revolving term of office, held in turn by each member state.

Finally, section 4 illustrated that even those measures which are agreed to will not necessarily have the effect anticipated. The slowness of some member states to transpose EC legislation into national law and the difficulty in ensuring that compliance meets both the spirit and the letter of the law will have implications for the impact of EC social policy in practice.

One of the most frustrating aspects of research on social policy at the European level is the lack of evidence on what has been achieved. We have explained in section 4 that much of the reason for this, even in areas where the task to be undertaken might appear fairly uniform (such as health and safety at work), is the lack of statistics and the inconsistency of what there is. As a result, cost benefit analyses of the kind we would like to see employed have never been developed. Such analyses would allow the evaluation of programmes against their intended outcomes - such as increasing employment, improving cohesion or improving conditions for target groups. Too often the form of assessment that has been used relates either to the expenditure of the money on the correct programmes in the designed location or to the measurement of inputs. However it is impossible to allocate scarce resources in an informed manner without knowing what return on the resources employed may be.

The work that we have carried out on assessment of EC-level social policy has therefore been principally qualitative, and focused on health and safety at work (Matthews, 1993); collective redundancies (Mayes and Soteri, 1994); posted workers (Gold, 1994); and European works councils (Hall et al., 1995).

Table 4.1 Progress in implementing directives applicable to employment and social policy

Member State	Directives applicable	Directives for which measures have been notified	%
Belgium	33	23	70
Denmark	33	30	91
Germany	34	23	68
Greece	33	23	70
Spain	33	23	70
France	33	27	82
Ireland	33	30	91
Italy	33	21	64
Luxembourg	33	20	61
Netherlands	33	23	70
Portugal	33	24	73
United Kingdom	33	32	97

Source: Commission of the EC (1993a).

Table 4.2 Enforcement powers of health and safety inspectorates in the UK, Germany, France and Italy

Powers	UK	Germany		France		Italy
		GAs	BGs	Labour inspect.	CRAMs	
Enter premises	•	•	•	•	•	•
Conduct inspections	•	•	•	•	•	•
Require relevant information	•	•	•	•		
Remove items	•					
Take samples	•			•	•	•
Copy documents	•					
Require specific measures	•	•	(a)	•	•	•
Order the suspension of dangerous work	•	•		(b)		
Initiate/refer cases for prosecution	•	•	•	•		•
Conduct prosecution	•					
Issue summary fines		•	•		(c)	
Close workplace		•				

Notes:
(a) Representatives of the Employers' Association Technical Committees in Germany cannot require specific measures to be taken, but may recommend improvements.
(b) The French Labour Inspectorate may apply for a court order to suspend dangerous work.
(c) Although prevention services of the sickness insurance funds in France may not issue fines, they may recommend the imposition of higher insurance premiums on a firm to take account of risk.
Source: Matthews (1993).

Table 4.3   Enforcement actions in the German Länder 1988-1990

Land	Year	Enforcement notices	Warnings	Fines	Cases referred	Successful prosecutions
Schleswig-Holstein	1990	54	8	15	2	0
	1989	57	5	21	0	0
	1988	55	15	20	3	0
Hamburg	1990	523	15	7	2	0
	1989	587	25	152	3	0
	1988	650	17	23	1	0
Niedersachsen	1990	686	75	108	11	13
	1989	593	139	155	21	38
	1988	514	83	144	11	18
Bremen	1990	32	16	34	0	1
	1989	25	22	59	0	1
	1988	46	5	2	2	0
Nordrhein Westfalen	1990	1171	184	278	86	16
	1989	1023	238	288	27	24
	1988	1211	304	365	20	19
Hessen	1990	223	95	71	8	27
	1989	201	88	135	7	7
	1988	260	65	84	3	9
Rheinland Pfalz	1990	577	34	85	2	•
	1989	554	34	108	2	•
	1988	408	25	56	4	•
Baden Württemberg	1990	280	•	•	2	0
	1989	192	•	•	10	0
	1988	205	•	•	4	2
Bayern	1990	4918	220	197	7	3
	1989	3862	443	320	3	7
	1988	3088	165	168	7	0
Saarland	1990	19	0	0	0	0
	1989	19	1	0	0	10
	1988	16	4	4	0	0
Berlin (West)	1990	1404	1126	43	2	4
	1989	356	905	38	4	17
	1988	351	1226	37	12	3

•Date not available.

Source: Arbeitssicherheit 1991. Unfallverhütungsbericht, Bundesministerium für Arbeit und Sozialordung.

References and Bibliography

Anderson (1988) 'Inadequate Implementation of EEC Directives: A Roadblock on the Way to 1992?', 11 Boston College International and Comparative Law Review 91, 96, No. 25.

Bachrach, P. and Baratz, M.S. (1970) 'Power and Poverty: Theory and Practice', New York: Oxford University Press.

Barrell, R.J. (1990) 'Has the EMS Changed Wage and Price Behaviour in Europe?', National Institute Economic Review, No. 133, November.

Barrell, R.J. (1994) 'Solvency and Cycles, or Lord, Make Us Good, But Not Yet', National Institute Discussion Paper, No. 65.

Begg, I. (1994) 'The Social Consequences of Economic and Monetary Union', Luxembourg: European Parliament.

Begg, I. and Mayes, D.G. (1994) 'The Impact of Peripherality for Northern Ireland', Report 111, Northern Ireland Economic Council.

Benington, J. (1991) 'The Integration of the Single European Market and State: Some Implications for Research, Policy Analysis and Development', draft report to the Joseph Rowntree Foundation, April, The Local Government Centre: University of Warwick.

Bertola, G. (1990) 'Job Security, Employment and Wages', European Economic Review, Vol. 34, pp. 851-886.

Borchardt, K.D. (1990) 'The ABC of Community Law', Luxembourg: Office for Offical Publications of the EC'.

Brewster, C. and Teague, P. (1989) 'European Community Social Policy' London: Institute of Personnel Management.

Breyer, S. (1979) 'Analysing Regulatory Failure', Harvard Law Review, Vol. 49.

Bridgford, J. & Stirling, J. (1991) 'Britain in a Social Europe: Industrial Relations and 1992', Industrial Relations Journal, Winter.

Budd, S. (1987) 'The EEC: a Guide to the Maze', London: Kogan Page.

Burridge M. and Mayes, D.G. (1993) 'A Single Currency for Europe by the Year 2000', Briefing Note No. 4, London: NIESR.

Butt Philip, A. (1988) 'The Application of the EEC Regulations on Drivers' Hours and Tachographs' in: Siedentopf, H. and Ziller, J. Making European Policies Work: The Implementation of Community Legislation in the Member States, Vol.I Comparative Syntheses, London: SAGE Publications.

Campbell, S. (1986) 'Labour Inspection in the European Community', London: HSE/HMSO.

Cole, R.J. and Tegeler, P.D. (1980) 'Government Requirements of Small Business', Lexington Massachussetts: Lexington Books.

Collins, D. (1975) 'The European Communities - The Social Policy of the First Phase: Volume Two The European Economic Community 1958-72', London: Martin Robertson.

Commission of the EC (1975) 'Employee Participation and Company Structure', Bulletin of the EC, Supplement 8/75, Brussels.

Commission of the EC (n.d.) 'Internal Conclusions Regarding Future Work, European Social Dialogue: Documentary Series', Brussels (no date: January 1989?).

Commission of the EC (1989) 'Communication from the Commission concerning its Action Programme relating to Implementation of the Community Charter of Basic Social Rights for Workers', COM(89) 568, Brussels.

Commission of the EC (1991a) 'Proposal for a Council Directive on the establishment of a European Works Council in Community-scale undertakings or groups of undertakings for the purposes of informing and consulting employees', COM(90) 581 final, Brussels.

Commission of the EC (1991b) 'The Pepper Report: the Promotion of Employee Participation in Profits and Enterprise Results', Social Europe Supplement, 1/92, Brussels.

Commission of the EC (1992a) Bulletin of the European Communities, Vol. 12.

Commission of the EC (1992b) 'Community Charter of the Fundamental Social Rights of Workers', in *Social Europe* 1/92, Brussels, pp. 7-11.

Commission of the EC (1992c) 'First Report on the Application of the European Community's Social Chapter', London Office Press Release ISEC/B1/92, pp. 3.

Commission of the EC (1993a) 'Tenth Annual Report on the Monitoring of the Application of Community Law 1992', Brussels.

Commission of the EC (1993b) 'Green Paper. European Social Policy: Options for the Union', COM(93) 551, 17 November, Brussels.

Commission of the EC (1993c) 'Growth, Competitiveness, Employment. The Challenges and Ways Forward into the 21st Century. White Paper', COM (93) 700 final, 5 December, Brussels.

Commission of the EC (1993d) 'Conclusions of the Presidency', Bulletin of the European Communities, Vol. 26, No. 12, Brussels.

Commission of the EC (1994a) 'European Social Policy - A Way Forward for the Union. A White Paper', COM(94) 333 final, 27 July, Brussels.

Commission of the EC (1994b) 'White Paper on European Social Policy - Key Proposals', Memo/94/55, 27 July, Brussels.

Commission of the EC (1994c) 'Employment in Europe', Brussels.

Committee for the Study of Economic and Monetary Union (Delors Committee) (1989) 'Report on Economic and Monetary Union in the European Community', April, Luxembourg.

Connerton, M. and MacCarthy, M. (1982) 'Cost/Benefit Analysis and Regulation: Expressway to Reform or Blind Alley?', Washington D.C.: Centre for National Policy.

Dehousse, R., Joerges, C., Majone, G., Snyder, F. with Everson, M. (1992) 'Europe after 1992: New Regulatory Strategies', European University Institute Working Paper in Law No. 92/31, Florence.

Due, J., Steen Madsen, J. & Stroby Jensen, C. (1991) 'The Social Dimension: Convergence or Divergence of Industrial Relations in the Single European Market?', Industrial Relations Journal, Summer.

Emerson, M. (1988) 'Regulation or Deregulation of the Labour Market: policy regimes for the recruitment and dismissal of employees in the industrialised countries', European Economic Review, Vol. 32, No. 4, pp. 775-817.

Emerson, M. et al (1988) 'The Economics of 1992: an Assessment of the Potential Economic Effects of Completing the Internal Market of the European Community', European Economy, No. 35.

Employment Department (1992) 'The United Kingdom in Europe. People, Jobs and Progress', September, London.

Employment Department/H M Treasury (1993) 'Growth, Competitiveness and Employment in the European Community, Paper by the United Kingdom', July, London.

Employment Department (1993) 'Social Affairs: the UK Presidency at Work', London: HMSO.

Employment Department (1994) 'European Commission's Green Paper on European Social Policy. The United Kingdom Response', April, London.

Employment Gazette (1991) 'EC backs British stance', May, p. 253.

Europe (1994), 'At Essen Summit Commission Proposes Guidelines Aimed at Strengthening the Fight against Unemployment - Five-Point Action Plan', 24 November, No. 6363 (new series).

European Economy (1991) Commission of the EC, Directorate General for Economic and Financial Affairs, March, No. 47.

Eurostat (1992) 'Methodology for the Harmonisation of European Occupational Accident Statistics', Luxembourg: Commission of the European Communities.

Ferner, A. (1988) 'Governments, Managers and Industrial Relations', Oxford: Blackwell.

Ferner, A. and Hyman, R. (eds.) (1992a) 'Industrial Relations in the New Europe', Oxford: Blackwell.

Ferner, A. and Hyman, R. (1992b) 'Industrial Relations in the New Europe: Seventeen Types of Ambiguity' in: Ferner, A. and Hyman, R. (eds.) (1992a), pp. xvi-xlix.

Fulcher, J. (1988) 'On the Explanation of Industrial Relations Diversity: Labour Movements, Employers and the State in Britain and Sweden', British Journal of Industrial Relations, 26,2.

Financial Times (1991) 'Maastricht Deal Lets UK Stay Out of Social Accord', 11 December, pp. 1.

Franzmeyer, F., Hrubesch, P., Seidel, B., Weise, C. and Schweiger, I. (1991) 'The Regional Impact of Community Policies', DIW, European Parliament Research Paper No. 19, Luxembourg: Office of Official Publications of the European Communities.

Freestone, D.A.C. and Davidson, J.S. (1988) 'The Institutional Framework of the European Communities', London: Croom Helm.

Gold, M. and Mayes, D. (1993) 'Rethinking a Social Policy for Europe' in: Simpson, R. and Walker, R. (eds.) 'Europe: for Richer or Poorer?', London: Child Poverty Action Group, pp. 25-38.

Gold, M. and Hall, M. (1994) 'Statutory European Works Councils: the Final Countdown?', Industrial Relations Journal, Vol. 25, No. 3, September, pp. 177-186.

Gold, M. (1994) 'The Impact of the Posted Workers' Directive on Company Practice in the UK', ED Research Series No. 37, London: Employment Department.

Gordon-Smith, D. (1989) 'The Drafting Process in the European Community', Statute Law Review.

Gregg, P. and Machin, S. (1994) 'Is the Rise in UK Inequality Different?' in Barrell, R. (ed.) The UK Labour Market, Cambridge: CUP.

Hager, W., Knight, A., Mayes, D.G. and Streeck, W. (1993), 'Public Interest and Market Pressures: Problems Posed by Europe 1992', London: Macmillan.

Hall, M. (1992) 'Legislating for Employee Participation: a Case Study of the European Works Councils Directive', Warwick Papers in Industrial Relations, No. 39, Industrial Relations Research Unit.

Hall, M., Carley, M., Gold, M., Marginson, P. and Sisson, K. (1995) 'The European Works Councils Directive - A Practical Guide', London: Industrial Relations Services.

Hartley, T.C. (1986) 'The Foundations of European Community Law', Oxford: Clarendon Press.

Hawkins, K. (1984) 'Environment and Enforcement: Regulation and Social Definition of Pollution' Oxford: Clarendon Press.

Health and Safety Executive (1991) 'Workplace Health and Safety in Europe', London: HMSO.

Health and Safety Executive (1994) 'The Costs to the British Economy of Work Accidents and Work-related Ill Health', Report by N.V. Davies and P. Teasdale, HSE Books.

Hepple, B. (1987) 'The Crisis in EEC Labour Law' Industrial Relations Law Journal.

Holloway, J. (1981) 'Social Policy Harmonisation in the European Community', Farnborough: Gower.

HM Treasury/Employment Department (1993) 'Growth, Competitiveness and Employment in the European Community', Paper by the United Kingdom for consideration by the Commission and Member States.

Hutter, B.M. (1989) 'Variations in Regulatory Enforcement Styles', Law and Policy, Vol. 11, No. 2, April.

Independent (1991) 'Maastricht: where Major made his big mistake', 13 December. p. 21.

James, P. (1993) 'The European Community: a Positive Force for Health and Safety?' in: Mayes, D. 'Aspects of European Integration', London: NIESR.

Krislov, Ehlermann and Weiler (1986) 'The Political Organs and the Decision-Making Process in the United States and the European Community' in: Cappelletti, Secombe and Weiler (eds) Integration through Law, Vol. 1: Methods, Tools and Institutions, Book 2: Political Organs, Integration Techniques and Judicial Process, Berlin: Walter de Gruyter.

Lindley, R.M. and Wilson, R.A. (1991) 'SEM Scenarios for the Employment of Women and Men in Great Britain', EOC/IER Seminar on the Implications of the Single European Market for the Employment of Women and Men in Great Britain, March, University of Warwick.

Lintner, V. and Mazey, S. (1991) 'The European Community: Economic and Political Aspects', London: McGraw-Hill.

Ludlow, P. (1991) 'The European Commission' in: Keohane, R.O. and Hoffman, S. The New European Community, Oxford: Westview Press.

McBarnet, D. (1992) 'It's Not What You Do But The Way That You Do It: Tax Evasion, Tax Avoidance and the Boundaries of Deviance' in: Downes, D. (ed.) Unravelling Criminal Justice, Basingstoke: Macmillan.

McBarnet, D. and Whelan, C. (1990) 'The Elusive Spirit of the Law: Formalism and the Struggle for Legal Control', Modern Law Review, 54, No. 6, November.

McBarnet, D. and Whelan, C. (1991) 'The Elusive Spirit of the Law: Formalism and the Struggle for Legal Control', Modern Law Review, November.

McBarnet, D. and Whelan, C. (1992) 'International Corporate Finance and the Challenge of Creative Compliance' in: Fingleton, J. (ed.) The Internationalisation of Capital Markets and the Regulatory Response, London: Graham and Trotman, pp. 129-141.

MacDougall, Sir D. (1977) 'Report of the Study Group on the Role of Public Finance in European Integration', Brussels: Commission of the European Communities.

McGarity, T.O. (1991) 'Reinventing Rationality', Cambridge: Cambridge University Press.

Matthews, D. (1992) 'The 1986 UK Presidency: an Assessment of its Impact on Social Policy Initiatives', ESRC SEM Programme Working Paper no. 10.

Matthews, D. (1993) 'Enforcement of Health and Safety Law in the UK, Germany, France and Italy', ESRC SEM Programme Working Paper no. 13.

Mayes, D.G. (1992) 'The Social and Labour Market Implications of 1992 for Scotland', ESRC SEM Programme Working Paper no. 8.

Mayes, D.G. (1993) 'Performance and Distribution' in: Hager, W., Knight, A., Mayes, D.G. and Streeck, W. 'Public Interest and Market Pressures: Problems Posed by Europe 1992', London: Macmillan.

Mayes, D.G. and Ogiwara, Y, (1992) 'Translating Japanese Success in the UK', National Institute Economic Review, No. 142.

Mayes, D.G. and Soteri, S. (1994) 'The Right of Dismissal and Labour Flexibility', Work Document No.121, The Hague: OSA.

Mazey, S. and Richardson, J. (1992) 'Interest Groups and European Integration', paper presented to the Political Studies Association Annual Conference, Belfast (7-9 April).

Meade, J.E. (1994) 'Full Employment without Inflation', London: Employment Policy Institute/Social Market Foundation.

Mosley, H. (1990) 'The Social Dimension of European Integration', International Labour Review.

Nam, C. and Reuter, J. (1991) 'The Impact of 1992 and Associated Legislation on the Less Favoured Regions of the European Community', European Parliament Working Documents, 18 EN-9-91.

National Institute of Economic and Social Research (1991) 'A Strategy for Social and Economic Cohesion after 1992', EP Briefing Paper No. 19, Luxembourg: Office for Official Publications of the European Communities.

National Institute of Economic and Social Research (1993) Unpublished Discussion Paper on Growth, Competitiveness and Employment prepared for the Department of Employment.

Olsen, P.B. (1992) 'Six Cultures of Regulation', Copenhagen: Handelshojskolen Forlag.

OECD (1989) 'Occupational Accidents in OECD Countries', Employment Outlook, July, Paris: OECD.

OECD (1994a) 'Jobs Study. Facts, Analysis, Strategies', Paris: OECD.

OECD (1994b) 'Assessing Structural Reform: Lessons for the Future', Paris: OECD.

Onofri, P. and Tomasini, S. (1992) 'France and Italy: a Tale of Two Adjustments' in: Barrell, R. (ed.) Economic Convergence and Monetary Union in Europe, London: Sage.

Padoa-Schioppa, T. (ed.) (1987) 'Efficiency, Stability and Equity: a Strategy for the Evolution of the Economic System of the European Community', Oxford: OUP.

Prais, S.J. et al. (1990) 'Productivity, Education and Training: Britain and Other Countries Compared', London: NIESR.

Richardson, G.M., Ogus, A.I. and Burrows, P. (1983) 'Policing Pollution: A Study of Regulation and Enforcement', Oxford: Clarendon Press.

Siedentopf, H. and Hauschild, C. (1988) 'The Implementation of European Union Legislation by the Member States: A Comparative Analysis' in: Siedentopf and Ziller (eds) Making European Policies Work, London: Sage.

Simpson, R. and Walker, R. (eds.) (1993) 'Europe: for Richer or Poorer?', London: Child Poverty Action Group.

Sisson, K., Waddington, J. and Whitston, C. (1992) 'The Structure of Capital in the European Community: the Size of Companies and the Implications for Industrial Relations', Warwick Papers in Industrial Relations, No. 38, Industrial Relations Research Unit.

Snyder, F. (1990) 'New Directions in European Community Law', London: Weidenfeld and Nicolson.

Snyder, F. (1993) 'The Effectiveness of European Community Law: Institutions, Processes, Tools and Techniques', 56 Modern Law Review 19.

Spiker, P. (1991) 'The Principle of Subsidiarity and the Social Policy of the EC', Journal of European Social Policy.

Streeck, W. (1987) 'The Uncertainties of Management in the Management of Uncertainty: Employers, Labour Relations and Industrial Adjustment in the 1980s', Work, Employment and Society, 1,3, pp. 281-308.

Sunday Times, (1994) 'British firms opt in to European works councils', 14 August, Section 3, Business.

Sutherland Report (1992) 'The Internal Market after 1992. Meeting the Challenge', Report to the EEC Commission by the High Level Group on the Operation of the Internal Market, Brussels.

Teague, P. (1989) 'The European Community: the Social Dimension', London: Kogan Page.

The Maastricht Treaty in Perspective - Consolidated Treaty on European Union (1992), British Management Data Foundation.

Vogel, D. (1986) 'National Styles of Regulation', Ithaca, USA: Cornell University Press.

von Prondzynski, F. (1992) 'Ireland: Between Centralism and the Market' in: Ferner, A. and Hyman,R. (eds.) (1992a), pp. 69-87.

Vranken, M. (1986) 'Deregulating the Employment Relationship: Current Trends in Europe', Comparative Labour Law Journal.

Walters, D.R. and Freeman, R.J. (1992) 'Employee Representation in Health and Safety at the Workplace: A Comparative Study in Five European Countries', Luxembourg: Office for Official Publications of the EC.

Weiler, J. (1991) 'The Transformation of Europe', 100 Yale Law Journal, 2463-2464.

Welsh, M. (1988) 'Labour Market Policy in the European Community: the British Presidency of 1986', London: Royal Institute of International Affairs.

Wilks, S. (1992) 'The Metamorphosis of European Community Policy', RUSEL Working Paper No. 9, University of Exeter.

Williams, S. (1991) 'Sovereignty and Accountability in the European Community' in Keohane, R. & Hoffman, S. The New European Community, Oxford: Westview Press.

Woolcock, S. (1994) 'The Single European Market: Centralisation or Competition among National Rules?' London: Royal Institute of International Affairs (European Programme).

Appendix I:
Update of EC Social and Labour Policy

Introduction

This table is divided into 13 sections, each one corresponding to the sections in the Commission's Social Action Programme.

I   Labour Market
II   Employment and Remuneration
III   Improvement of Living and Working Conditions
IV   Freedom of Movement
V   Social Protection
VI   Association and Collective Bargaining
VII   Information, Consultation and Participation
VIII Equal Treatment for Men and Women
IX   Vocational Training
X   Health and Safety
XI   Protection of Children and Adolescents
XII   The Elderly
XIII The Disabled
Miscellaneous provisions

Each of these 13 sections is subdivided into:
a) a selection of those measures pre-dating the Social Action Programme
b) those measures contained within the Social Action Programme

In this way, the reader can more easily assess the focus of EC social and labour policy and trace the relationship of measures over time.

There are four columns:

-   Subject: the official title or brief description of the measure concerned, in each case with an Official Journal (OJ) of the EC reference (either C series for Communications or L series for Legislation)

-   Base: the legal base or Article in the EEC Treaty on which the measure has been introduced, where relevant

-   Date: the date on which the measure was either first adopted by the Commission or submitted by it to the Council, where known - official sources vary as to which date is given (sometimes several months can elapse between the two), but here we have tried to give the adoption date, in line with practice in the *Bulletin of the European Communitie*s. Where a second date is given as well, this refers to the adoption of the amended proposal

-   Current position: an outline of the stage reached by the measure (dates in this column refer to the one on which it was formally adopted by the Council, unless otherwise indicated).

The information is accurate, as far as we are aware, as on 1 December 1994. However, the *Bulletin of the European Communities* - currently published ten times a year by the Commission of the EC - provides the definitive version. So far, the Social Protocol has been invoked in relation to Directives governing European works councils, parental leave, burden of proof and non-standard forms of employment ("atypical work").

I Labour Market

Subject	Base	Date	Current position
Regulation 1612/68 on the movement of workers within the Community (OJL257/68).			Revised by Council 27/07/92 freedom of *(see below)*.
Resolution on unemployment amongst women (OJ C161/84).		16/11/83	Adopted 07/06/84.
Resolution on local employment initiatives (OJ C161/84).		21/11/83	Adopted 07/06/84.
Resolution on action to combat long-term unemployment (OJ C2/85).		14/09/84	Adopted 13/12/84.

I Labour Market *(continued)*

Subject	Base	Date	Current position
Programme for specific employment measures (OJ C165/85).			Adopted 13/06/85.
Resolution on action programme on employment growth (OJ C340/86).			Adopted 11/12/86.
Resolution to assist the long-term unemployed (OJ C157/90).			Adopted 29/05/90.
Resolution to combat unemployment (OJ C ref. still to appear).			Council Resolution adopted 03/12/92.

Social Action Programme Initiatives

Subject	Base	Date	Current position
"Employment in Europe" Report: 1994 edition COM(94)381.			Commission Report "Employment in Europe" has appeared annually since 1989. The sixth issue, for 1994, been adopted by the Commission.
"Observatory" and documentation system on employment.			The "observatory" is a term embracing three separate initiatives: i) MISEP, the quarterly newsletter of the Mutual Information System on Employment Policies. ii) SYSDEM, the quarterly publication of the European System of Documentation on Employment (began 1990). iii) NEC, the Network of Employment Co-ordinators, which produces research reports on themes (such as skills shortages in particular sectors).
Action programmes on employment creation for specific target groups.			These include: i) ERGO: a programme for the long-term unemployed, which has been running for three years (1989-91). ii) LEDA: a programme to promote local employment initiatives, which has been running since 1986 and is currently in phase III (1990-93). iii) SPEC: a special programme for employment creation which began in 1990.

Social Action Programme Initiatives *(continued)*

Subject	Base	Date	Current position
			iv) ELISE: European information network on local employment initiatives (since 1985).
Regulation no. 2434/92 amending Part II of Regulation No 1612/68 on freedom of movement for workers within the Community (OJ L245/92).	(49)	12/09/91	Concerns revision of the European system for the international clearance of vacancies and applications for employment (Systeme europeen de diffusion des offres et demandes d'emploi en compensation: SEDOC - now known as Eures). Adopted by Council 27/07/92.
Monitoring and evaluation of the activities of the European Social Fund.			Ongoing evaluation - Annual Report on the Implementation of Reform of the Structural Funds.
Proposed Directive amending Directive (EEC) No.68/360 on the abolition of restrictions on movement and residence within the Community for workers of member states and their families (OJ C100/89).		09/04/90 (amended)	No details available.

II Employment and Remuneration: Social Action Programme Initiatives Only

Subject	Base	Date	Current position
Proposed Council Directive on non-standard employment (original proposals published in OJ C224/90 and, as amended, OJ C305/90) New Belgian text not yet available.	(100)	29/06/90, 07/11/90 (amended)	This is the result of a merger of the two 'atypical work' draft Directives submitted in June 1990. The Belgian Presidency held discussions on the new text at the Councils on 12/10/93 and 23/11/93. It was discussed again on 19/04/94 (Greek Presidency). Adopted under the Social Protocol in December 1994.
'Atypical work': Directive on improving the health and safety at work of temporary workers (OJ L206/91).	(118A)	13/06/90 07/11/90 (amended)	Final adoption by Council 25/06/91; implementation by 31/12/92.
Opinion on the introduction of an equitable wage by the member states (OJ C248/93).	(118)	11/12/91	Adopted by Commission, 01/09/93.

III Improvement of Living and Working Conditions

Subject	Base	Date	Current position
Directive on procedures to be applied in redundancy situations (OJ L48/75).			Adopted 19/02/75; implementation required by 12/02/76.
Recommendation on the principle of a 40-hour week and four weeks' annual paid holiday (OJ L199/75).			Adopted 23/07/75; implementation required by 31/12/78.
Directive on employees' rights and advantages in mergers and takeovers (transfer of undertakings) (OJ L61/77).			Adopted 16/02/77; implementation required by 16/02/79. Amendments now under discussion in the Commission.
Directive on the protection of employees in the event of their employers' insolvency (OJ L283/80).			Adopted 22/10/80; implementation required by 22/10/83.
Recommendation on Community policy regarding retirement age (OJ L357/82).		15/12/81	Adopted 10/12/82; first progress reports required by June 1985.
Proposed Recommendation on reduction and reorganisation of working time (OJ C290/83).		16/09/83	Vetoed at Council meeting on 07/06/84 by the UK.
Proposed Directive amending 1977 Directive on transfer of undertakings (No OJ reference available).	100	Dec. 1992	Commission published preliminary consultation document in Dec. 1992. Social partners were consulted in March 1994. Proposal not yet published.

Social Programme Initiatives

Subject	Base	Date	Current position
Directive on an employers' obligation to inform employees on the conditions applicable to the contract of employment relationship (OJ L288/91).	(100)	28/11/90 26/07/91 (amended)	Final adoption by Council on 14/10/91 Implementation by 30/06/93.
Directive concerning certain aspects of the organisation of working time (OJ L307/93).	(118A)	03/08/90 23/04/91 (amended)	Adopted in principle by Council on 24/06/92, though technical disagreements deferred final adoption till 23/11/93. Numerous exemptions on some provisions.

Social Programme Initiatives (continued)

Subject	Base	Date	Current position
Proposed Revision of Council Directive 75/129/ EEC of 17 February 1975 on the approximation of the laws of the member states pertaining to collective redundancies (OJ C310/91; amended OJ C117/92; L ref. still to appear).	(100)	18/09/91 31/03/92 (amended)	Formal adoption by Council 24/06/92.
Memorandum on the social integration of migrants from non-member countries.		28/09/90	

IV Freedom of Movement

Subject	Base	Date	Current position
Regulation 1251/70 on the right of workers to remain in the territory of a member state after having been employed in that member state (OJ L242/70).			Currently being revised by the Commission (see below).
Decision on exchange of young workers within the Community (OJ C153/84).			Adopted 13/12/84.

Social Action Programme Initiatives

Subject	Base	Date	Current position
Revision of Commission Regulation (EEC) 1251/70 of 29 June 1970 on the right of workers to remain on the territory of a member state after having been employed in that state.			Depends on the adoption of revision of Part I of Regulation (EEC) no.1612/68 (See section 1).
Proposal for a Regulation (51,235) extending Council Regulation (EEC)1408/71 on the application of social security schemes to employed persons, to self-employed persons and to members of their families moving within the Community and Council Regulation (EEC) 574/72 (laying down the procedure for implementing Regulation 1408/71) to all insured persons (OJ C221/90, amended OJ C219/91, amended OJ C46/92).		24/07/90 23/07/91 (amended)	Endorsed by EP 11/10/91 and by ESC 26/02/92.

Social Action Programme Initiatives *(continued)*

Subject	Base	Date	Current position
Proposed Directive concerning the posting of workers in the framework of the provision of services (OJ C225/91, amended OJ C187/93).	(57(2), 66)	28/06/91 15/06/93 (amended)	Discussed in Council 03/12/92 and 23/11/93. Disagreements but draft prioritised by German Presidency.
Proposal for a Community instrument on the introduction of a labour clause into public contracts.			The subject of this proposal has been merged into the posted workers' Directive (above).
Proposed Resolution on supplementary social security schemes: the role of occupational pension schemes in the social protection of workers and their implications for freedom of movement.		18/07/91	Discussed by Council 03/12/92.
Communication on the living and working conditions of Community citizens residing in frontier regions and of frontier workers in particular.		27/11/90	

V Social Protection

Subject	Base	Date	Current position
Recommendation on social security for voluntary development workers (OJ L163/85).		12/12/84	Adopted 13/06/85.

Social Action Programme Initiatives

Subject	Base	Date	Current position
Recommendation on the convergence of social protection objectives and policies (OJ L245/92).	(235)	27/06/91	Adopted by Council 27/07/92 .
Recommendation on common criteria concerning sufficient resources and social assistance in the social protection systems (OJ C163/91; OJ L ref. still to appear).	(235)	13/05/91	Adopted by Council 24/06/92.

VI Association and Collective Bargaining: Social Action Programme Initiatives only

Subject	Base	Date	Current position
Communication on the role of the social partners in collective bargaining.			

VII Information, consultation and participation

Subject	Base	Date	Current position
Proposed Fifth Directive on company structure and administration (OJ C131/72, amended OJ C240/83).		1972 Aug 1983	Ongoing discussions - future linked to that of the European Company Statute.
Proposed Directive on procedures for informing and consulting employees in large national and multinational firms ("Vredeling" Directive) (OJ C297/80, amended OJ C217/83).		24/10/80 15/06/83 (amended)	Council Conclusion, adopted 21/07/86, froze all further discussion till 1989. Since then, the proposal has been overtaken by the draft European Works Councils Directive.
Proposed Regulation and Directive on the Statute for a European Company (OJ C263/89, amended OJ C176/91).	(100A) Reg, 54(2) Dir.	Aug 1989 16/05/91 (amended)	Original proposals date back to proposed Regulation of May 1975 (OJ C93/74, OJ C124/74) Discussed at meeting of internal market Council on 16/12/93.
[See also details of proposed Statutes governing the non-profit making sectors under Miscellaneous, below.]			

Social Action Programme Initiatives

Subject	Base	Date	Current position
Directive on the establishment of a European Works Council in Community-scale undertakings or groups of undertakings for the purposes of informing and consulting employees (OJ C199/94).	(100)	12/12/90 16/09/91 (amended)	After controversial debates, this measure was adopted in Council on 22/09/94 *Applies to 11 member states only.*
Recommendation concerning the promotion of employee participation in profits and enterprise results (PEPPER) (OJ L245/92).	(235)	09/07/91 05/05/92 (amended)	Formally adopted by Council 27/07/92.

VIII Equal treatment for men and women

Subject	Base	Date	Current position
Directive on equal pay for men and women (OJ L45/75).			Adopted 12/02/75 Implementation by 12/02/76.
Directive on equal treatment for men and women as regards access to employment, promotion vocational training and working conditions (OJ L39/76).			Adopted 12/02/76 Implementation by 12/08/78.
Directive on equal treatment for men and women in state social security (OJ L6/79).			Adopted 22/12/78 Implementation by 22/12/84.
First Community programme on equal opportunities for women and men (OJ C186/82).			Resolution adopted 27/05/82.
Directive on equal treatment for men and women in occupational social security schemes (OJ L225/86).		05/05/83	Adopted 21/07/86 Implementation by 01/01/93.
Proposed Directive on parental leave and leave for family reasons (OJ C333/83 and, as amended, OJ C316/84).	100	24/11/83, 15/11/84	Amended draft submitted to Council in Nov.1984. Revived by Belgian Presidency, discussed in Council 23/11/93. At Council on 19/04/94 Commission announced it would use Social Protocol procedure.
Directive on equal treatment for men and women engaged in a self-employed capacity and on protection of self-employed women during pregnancy (OJ L359/86).		15/03/84	Adopted 11/12/86.
Recommendation on the promotion of positive action for women (OJ L331/84).		26/04/84	Adopted 13/12/84.
Second Community programme on equal opportunities for women and men 1986-1990 (OJ C203/86).		Dec 1985	Resolution adopted 05/06/86.
Proposed Directive on completion of equal treatment in social security (OJ C309/87).		27/10/87	Covers pension age, survivors' benefits and family allowances; Council meeting in June 1989 referred it back to COREPER.
Proposed Directive on the burden of proof (OJ C176/88).	119	27/05/88	Revived by the Belgian Presidency and discussed on Council 23/11/93 At Council on 19/04/94, Commission announced it would use Social Protocol procedure.

VIII Equal treatment for men and women *(continued)*

Subject	Base	Date	Current position
Resolution on the protection of the dignity of women and men at work (OJ C157/90).			Adopted 29/05/90 (Recommendation and Code of Practice adopted by Council 27/11/91 - *see below*.)

Social Action Programme Initiatives

Subject	Base	Date	Current position
Directive concerning measures to encourage improvements in the safety and health of pregnant workers, women workers who have recently given birth and women who are breastfeeding (L348/92).	(118A)	18/09/90 08/01/91 (amended)	Formal adoption by Council 19/10/92 Implementation by 19/10/94.
Council Resolution on the third medium-term Community action programme on equal opportunities for women and men, 1991-1995 (OJ C142/91).	(119)	17/10/90	Resolution adopted 21/05/91.
Recommendation concerning childcare (OJ L123/92).	(235)	08/07/91	Proposal submittted under the terms of the third action programme on equal opportunities Agreed in principle on Council 03/12/91; adopted by Council 31/03/92.
Proposed Recommendation concerning a code of good conduct on the protection of pregnancy and maternity.			Work to begin once Directive on pregnant workers adopted (see above).
Recommendation and Code of Practice on the protection of the dignity of women and men at work (OJ L49/92); Council Declaration (OJ C27/92).	(235)	03/07/91	Proposal submitted under the terms of the third action programme on equal opportunities as requested by Council in its Resolution of 29/05/90 Adopted by Council 27/11/91, and accompanying Declaration formally adopted 19/12/91.

IX Vocational training

Subject	Base	Date	Current position
Resolution on training and new information technology (OJ C166/83).		10/06/82	Adopted 02/06/83.
Resolution on training in the 1980s (OJ C193/83.		28/10/82	Adopted 03/06/83.

IX Vocational training *(continued)*

Subject	Base	Date	Current position
Decision adopting an action programme for the training and preparation of young people for adult and working life (OJ L346/87).		March 1987	Adopted 01/12/87.
Recommendation on vocational training for women (OJ L342/87).		April 1987	Adopted 24/11/87.
Council Directive on a general system for the recognition of higher education diplomas awarded on completion of professional education and training of at least three years' duration (OJ L19/89).		1985	Adopted 21/12/88.
Directive on a second general system for the recognition of professional education and training which complements Directive 89/48 (EEC) (OJ L209/92).		26/07/89 08/08/90 (amended)	Adopted by Council 18/06/92.
Community action programme for the development of continuing vocational training 1991-1994 (FORCE) (OJ L156/90).		15/11/89 26/04/90 (amended)	Drafted in response to Council Resolution of 07/06/89; adopted by Council 29/05/90 .
Second Community action programme to promote innovation in the field of vocational training and technological change 1990-1994 (Eurotecnet II) (OJ L393/89). [Eurotecnet I covered 1985-1988]			Adoption by Council 18/12/89.
Community initiatives (OJ C327/90): - for the development of new qualifications, new skills and new employment oppportunities (Euroform).		18/07/90	Adopted by Council 18/12/90.
- for the promotion of equal opportunities for women in the field of employment and vocational training (NOW).		18/07/90	Adopted by Council 18/12/90.
- concerning handicapped persons and certain other disadvantaged groups (Horizon).		18/07/90	Adopted by Council 18/12/90.

IX Vocational training (continued)

Subject	Base	Date	Current position
Resolution on the "transparency" of vocational qualifications (OJ C ref. still to appear).			Council Resolution adopted 03/12/92.
Proposed Council Decision establishing an action programme for the implementation of an EC vocational training policy (LEONARDO) (OJ C67/94, amended OJ C176/94.	127	04/02/94	'Common position' reached by Council on 22/06/94.

Social Action Programme Initiatives

Subject	Base	Date	Current position
Proposed Community instrument on access to vocational training.			Advisory Committee on Vocational Training consulted in early June 1992. A proposed Decision may be published.
Updating of the 1963 proposed Council Decision on the general principles for implementing a common vocational training policy.			
Communication on the rationalisation and co-ordination of vocational training programmes at Community level (Social Europe 3/90).	128	21/08/90	Community vocational training programmes to be grouped into three areas: - initial training - higher education - continuing training.
Proposal concerning the joint programme for the exchange of young workers and youth exchanges.			Adopted by Council 29/05/90; Council wishes to synchronise this programme with the "Youth for Europe" programme and PETRA II (see below).
Resolution on the Comparability of vocational training qualifications (OJ C109/91).			Formally adopted by Council 18/05/90.
PETRA action programme for vocational training of young people and their preparation for adult and working life: First phase (1988-1991).			Decision adopted 01/12/87.
Second phase (1992-1994) (OJ L214/91).		10/10/90 24/06/91 (amended)	Decision formally adopted 22/07/91 (PETRA II incorporates "exchange of young workers" programme.

Social Action Programme Initiatives *(continued)*

Subject	Base	Date	Current position
Decision adopting an action programme to promote youth exchanges and mobility in the Community: the "youth for Europe" Programme (OJ C308/90 and, as amended, OJ C175/91).		10/10/90 05/06/91 (amended)	Adopted by Council 26/06/91.

X Health and Safety

Subject	Base	Date	Current position
Directive on classification, packaging and labelling of dangerous substances (OJ L259/79).			Originally adopted in 1967, this Directive has been subject to a series of amendments - the sixth was notified to member states in September 1979 and the seventh is currently under discussion
Directive on protection for use of electrical equipment in potentially explosive atmospheres (OJ L24/76, OJ L43/79).			Framework Directive adopted in 1976 and special implementing Directive adopted 06/02/79; implementation by 06/08/80.
Directive on safety signs at the workplace (0J L229/77 and, as amended, OJ L183/79).			Originally adopted in 1977, this Directive was amended in June 1979; Implementation by 01/01/81.
First Community Programme on safety (OJ C165/78).			Resolution adopted 29/06/78.
Directive on the protection of workers exposed to vinyl chloride monomer risks (OJ L197/78).			Adopted 29/06/78. Implementation by 29/12/79.
Directive on major accident hazards of certain industrial activities (OJ L230/82).		July 1979 June 1981 (amended)	Formally adopted 25/06/82 Implementation by 08/01/84.
Directive on the protection of workers exposed to lead risks (OJ L247/82).		Dec 1979	Formally adopted 27/07/82. Implementation by 01/01/86.
Euratom Directive on the protection of workers exposed to radiation risks (OJ L246/80).			Adopted 15/07/80. Implementation by 03/12/82.
Directive on the protection of workers exposed to asbestos risks (OJ L263/83).		Sept 1980	Formally adopted 19/09/83. Implementation by 01/01/87 or by 01/01/90 for asbestos mining.

Subject	Base	Date	Current position
Directive on the marketing and use of asbestos (OJ L263/83).		1980	Formally adopted 19/09/83. Implementation by March 1986.
Directive on the protection of workers from harmful exposure to chemical, physical and biological agents at work (OJ L327/80).			Adopted 27/11/80. Implementation by 04/12/84.
Directive on the protection of workers exposed to noise risks (OJ L137/86).		18/10/82 23/07/84 (amended)	Formally adopted 12/05/86. Implementation by 01/01/90.
Second Community programme on safety and health at work (OJ C67/84).			Resolution formally adopted 27/02/84.
Directive on protection of workers by the banning of certain specified agents and/ or work activities (OJ L179/88).		1984	Adopted 09/06/88. Implementation by 01/01/90.
Directive amending 1980 Directive on the protection of workers related to exposure to chemical, physical and biological agents at work (OJ L356/88).		09/06/86	Formal adoption 16/12/88.
Third Community programme on safety, hygiene and health at work (OJ C28/88).			Resolution adopted 21/12/87.
"Framework" Directive on the introduction of measures to encourage improvements in the safety and health of workers at the workplace (OJ L183/89).		11/03/88	Adopted 12/06/89. Article 16(1) of this framework Directive permits the inclusion of further individual Directives within its remit. Implementation from 01/01/93.
(1) Directive on minimum safety and health requirements for the workplace (OJ L393/89).		11/03/88	Formal adoption 30/11/89. Implementation from 01/01/93.
(2) Directive on minimum safety and health requirements for the use of work equipment by workers at work (OJ L393/89).		11/03/88	Formal adoption 30/11/89. Implementation from 01/01/93.
(3) Directive on minimum safety and health requirements for the use by workers of personal protective equipment (OJ L393/89).		11/03/88	Formal adoption 30/11/89. Implementation from 01/01/93.

Subject	Base	Date	Current position
(4) Directive on minimum safety and health requirements for the manual handling of loads where there is a risk particularly of back injury for workers (OJ L156/90).		11/03/88 06/04/90 (amended)	Formal adoption 29/05/90. Implementation from 01/01/93.
(5) Directive on minimum safety and health requirements for work with display screen equipment (OJ L156/90).		11/03/88 22/05/90 (amended)	Formal adoption 29/05/90. Implementation from 01/01/93.
(6) Directive on the protection of workers exposed to carcinogens at work (OJ L196/90).		21/12/87 22/05/90 (amended)	Formal adoption 28/06/90. Implementation from 01/01/93.
(7) Directive on the protection of workers from the risks related to exposure to biological agents at work (OJ L374/90).		19/04/88	Formal adoption 26/11/90. Implementation from 26/11/93.
Proposed Directive to amend Directive (7) on biological agents (OJ C217/92).		15/07/92	Under discussion.

Social Action Programme Initiatives

Subject	Base	Date	Current position

Directive on "atypical" workers: see section II above (Employment and Remuneration).

Directive on working time: see section III above (Improvement of Living and Working Conditions).

Directive on pregnant workers: see section VIII above (Equal Treatment for Men and Women).

Subject	Base	Date	Current position
(8) Directive on the implementation of minimum safety and health requirements at temporary or mobile work sites (OJ L245/92).	(118A)	31/07/90 09/04/91 (amended)	Formal adoption 24/06/92. Implementation from 01/01/94.
(9) Directive on the minimum requirements for safety and/or health signs at work (OJ L245/92).	(118A)	21/12/90 11/06/92 (amended)	Amended and redrafted version of the 1977 Directive on safety signs at the workplace. Formal adoption 24/06/92 Implementation from 24/06/94 (longer for existing signs).
(10) Proposed Directive on the minimum safety and health requirements for work on board fishing vessels (OJ C337/91).	(118A)	03/12/91	ESC Opinion 29/04/92, EP first reading 08/07/92.

Social Action Programme Initiatives *(continued)*

Subject	Base	Date	Current position
(11) Directive concerning minimum requirements for improving the safety and health protection of workers in the mineral-extracting industries through drilling (OJ C46/92; OJ L ref. still to appear).	(118A)	19/12/91 07/08/92 (amended)	Formal adoption 03/11/92. Implementation two years from adoption.
(12) Directive concerning minimum requirements for improving the safety and health of workers in the extractive industries for the exploration and exploitation of minerals in mines and quarries (OJ C58/92 and, as amended, OJ C171/92; OJ L ref. still to appear).	(118A)	17/02/92 09/06/92 (amended)	Formal adoption 03/12/92.
Directive on the minimum safety and health requirements. for improved medical treatment on board vessels (OJ L113/92).	(118A)	24/07/90 28/02/91 (amended)	Formal adoption 31/03/92. Implementation from 01/01/95.
Directive amending 1983 Directive on the protection of workers from the risks related to exposure to asbestos at work (OJ L206/91).	(118A)	12/06/90	Formal adoption 25/06/91. Implementation from 01/01/93. (later for asbestos mining and for Greece).
Recommendation to the member states on a European schedule of industrial diseases (OJ L160/90).		22/05/90	This Recommendation updates a schedule of industrial diseases liable to compensation and subject to preventative measures established following Recommendations in 1962 and 1966.
Proposed Directive on the protection of the health and safety of workers from the risks related to chemical agents at work (OJ C165/93, amended OJ C191/94).	118A	17/05/93, 09/06/94 (amended)	Progress reported to Council 22/06/94.
Proposed Directive on the minimum safety and health requirements regarding the exposure of workers to the risks arising from physical agents (OJ C77/93).	118A	08/02/93 08/07/94 (amended)	No progress since submission of amended version.

Social Action Programme Initiatives *(continued)*

Subject	Base	Date	Current position
Proposed Directive on the minimum safety and health requirements for transport activities and workplaces on means of transport (OJ C25/93, and as amended, OJ C294/93).	118A	17/11/92, 01/10/93 (amended)	No progress since submission of amended version.
Proposed Regulation establishing a European Agency for safety and health at work (OJ C271/91).	(235)	30/09/91	European Council, 29/10/93, confirmed Agency would be set up in Bilbao, Spain. Political agreement on Council 22/06/94.
Proposed Directive amending Directive 89/655/EEC on the minimum health and safety requirements for the use of work equipment by workers (OJ C104/94).	(118A)	14/03/94	

XI Protection of Children and Adolescents

Social Action Programme Initiatives only

Subject	Base	Date	Current position
Directive on the protection of young people at work (OJ C84/92, as amended, OJ C77/93).	(118A)	18/03/92	Final adoption by Council 22/06/94. Implementation required within two years (exemptions for UK on certain provisions).

XII The Elderly

Social Action Programme Initiatives only

Subject	Base	Date	Current position
Communication and a Decision concerning the elderly (OJ L28/91).	(235)	24/04/90	Adopted by the Council 26/11/90.

XIII The Disabled

Subject	Base	Date	Current position
Community Programme for the disabled for 1983-1987 (OJ C347/81).			Adopted 08/12/81; Report on implementation published July 1987.
Recommendation on the employment of disabled people in the Community (OJ L225/86).		24/01/86	Adopted 05/06/86.

XIII The Disabled *(continued)*

Subject	Base	Date	Current position
Community Action Programme for the disabled (HELIOS I) for 1988-1991 (OJ L104/88; OJ L192/88; Council Conclusions OJ C173/89).		24/07/87	Decision adopted 18/04/88 and amplified by Council Conclusions of June 1988. Council Decision of 18/12/89 ensured continuation of Handynet 1990-1992 (computer- ised information system on disability). Report on the HELIOS I programme adopted by the Commission 06/07/92.

Social Action Programme Initiatives

Subject	Base	Date	Current position
Proposed Decision establishing a third	(128, 235)	08/10/91	Endorsed by ESC 29/01/92 Discussed by Council.
Community Programme for disabled people for 1992-1996 (HELIOS II) (OJ C293/91).		03/12/92	
Proposed Directive on the minimum requirements to improve the mobility and safe transport to work of workers with reduced mobility (OJ C68/91, amended OJ C15/92).	(118A)	11/02/91 20/12/91 (amended)	ESC Opinion 29/05/91. EP Opinion 20/11/91.

Miscellaneous Provisions (outside Social Charter)

Subject	Base	Date	Current position
Social Action Programme (OJ C13/74).			The first social action programme was adopted by a Resolution in February 1974.
Action programmes on poverty: - First programme 1975-1980.			Decision adopted.
- Second programme 13/12/84 1985-1988 (OJ L2/85).			Decision adopted.
- Third programme 1989-1993 (OJ C60/89).		03/01/89	Decision adopted.
Resolution of the Councils and Representatives of Governments on the fight against racism and xenophobia (C157/90).			Resolution adopted 29/05/90.

Miscellaneos Provisions (outside Social Charter) *(continued)*

Subject	Base	Date	Current position
Comparative assessment of the legal instruments implemented in the various member states to combat all forms of discrimination, racism and xenophobia and incitement to hatred and racial violence (OJ C157/90).			
Proposed Statutes for a European Association, Co-operative Society and Mutual Society (OJ C99/92, amended OJ C236/93).	100A Reg, 54(2) Directives	06/03/92 06/07/93 (amended)	Progress reported at internal market Council, 16/12/93. Drafts relating to co-operative societies discussed further on 16/06/94.

Appendix II:
Work completed for the
Department of Employment

Single European Market (SEM) Working Papers:

The Social and Labour Market Implications of 1992 for Scotland, No. 8, David Mayes (Oct. 1992).

The 1986 UK Presidency: an Assessment of its Impact on Social Policy Initiatives, No. 10, Duncan Matthews (Oct. 1992).

EC Social and Labour Policy: an Overview and Update, No. 11, Michael Gold (Dec. 1992).

The Development of EC Social Dialogue, No. 12, Michael Gold (Dec. 1992).

Enforcement of Health and Safety Law in the UK, Germany, France and Italy, No. 13, Duncan Matthews (May 1993).

Assessing the Effectiveness of Regulatory Enforcement: the Case of Occupational Accident Statistics in the European Community, No. 18, Duncan Matthews (Feb. 1994).

The Evolution of European Community Policy on the Mutual Recognition of Professional Qualifications, No. 19, Duncan Matthews (June 1994).

Ensuring the Effective Implementation, Enforcement and Compliance of European Community Law, No. 20, Duncan Matthews (June 1994).

Other Publications

Social Policy: the UK and Maastricht, Michael Gold, *National Institute Economic Review*, No. 139 (Feb. 1992).

The 1992 UK Presidency of the Council of Ministers, Duncan Matthews and David Mayes, *National Institute Economic Review*, No. 141 (Aug. 1992).

Balancing the Single Act, Michael Gold, *Parliamentary Brief*, Vol. 1 (Nov. 1992).

The Formulation of EC Social Policy - Preparatory Stages, Michael Gold, in: *Aspects of European Integration*, ed. David Mayes (London: NIESR, 1993).

EC Health and Safety Policy - Better Safe than Sorry, Michael Gold and Duncan Matthews, *European Business Journal*, Vol. 5, No. 4 (1993).

Helping the Workers, But Not the Workless, Duncan Matthews, *European Brief*, Vol. 2, No. 1 (October/November 1994).

Reports

The Impact of the Posted Workers' Directive on Company Practice in the UK, ED Research Brief, Michael Gold (1994: forthcoming).

Unpublished papers

Discussion Paper on Growth, Competitiveness and Employment, National Institute of Economic and Social Research (Dec. 1993) .

Conference and seminar papers

The Impact of European Integration on the UK Labour Market: a Research Strategy, Duncan Matthews, at *Joint NWO-ESRC Workshop on the Single Market*, Wageningen, Netherlands (11/12 Nov. 1991).

The Single European Market and its Implications for Social Policy Research, David Mayes, at *Joseph Rowntree Foundation Workshop*, University of Warwick (14 January 1992).

Europe: the Impact on Expatriation, Michael Gold, at *Managing Relocation*, CBI Conference, Liverpool (1 April 1992).

The Social and Labour Market Implications of 1992, David Mayes, at *Royal Society of Edinburgh*, Edinburgh (8 Sept. 1992).

The Formulation of EC Social Policy - Preparatory Stages, Michael Gold, at *Joint NWO-ESRC Workshop on the Single European Market*, Wiston House, Sussex (7/8 Oct. 1992).

Is there a Model of European Industrial Relations?, Michael Gold, Initiatives in *Employee Relations: Ideals and Realities*, St Edmund Hall, Oxford (4/6 April 1993).

Enforcing Health and Safety Law in Four Member States, Duncan Matthews, at *Joint NWO-ESRC Workshop on the Single European Market*, Noordwijk, Netherlands (27/28 Oct. 1993)

Social Regulation: Continuity or Convergence, Michael Gold, at *Royal Institute of International Affairs Study Group on Competition among Rules*, RIIA, London (25 Nov. 1993).

Social Partnership at European Community Level, Michael Gold, at *ESRC Research Seminar: State Autonomy in the European Community*, Centre for European Politics, Economy and Society, University of Oxford (14/15 Jan. 1994).

Impact of EC Policies on Employment, Michael Gold, at a series of *European Social Policy Seminars* organised by the Civil Service College, Sunningdale Park (18 Mar. 1992; 27 Nov. 1992; 29 Oct. 1993; 18 Jan. 1994; and 12 Dec. 1994).

Employment Department Seminars

European Works Councils: Michael Gold (11 Dec. 1991).

The 1986 UK Presidency: an Assessment of its Impact on Social Policy Initiatives: Duncan Matthews (27 March 1992).

EC Social and Labour Policy - an Overview and Update: Michael Gold (5 May 1992).

Policy Formulation in the EC - Determination in the Early Stages: Michael Gold (9 June 1992).

The Development of Consultation and Negotiation between Employers and Workers at EC Intersectoral, Sectoral and Company Level: Michael Gold (23 July 1992).

A Comparison of Enforcement Regimes - Health and Safety Legislation in France, Germany, Italy and the UK: Duncan Matthews (19 May 1993).

The Impact of the Posted Workers' Directive on Company Practice in the UK: Michael Gold (12 April 1994).

Enforcement and Compliance in the EC: Duncan Matthews (6 June 1994).

The Draft European Works Councils Directive - its Impact on the UK: Michael Gold (18 October 1994).

Further Work

Michael Gold also completed a project on communications in multinational companies financed by the European Foundation for the Improvement of Living and Working Conditions (Dublin) at the same time as working on the Department of Employment project. This resulted in a series of conference papers and publications, the most important of which are:

'Experiences with Decentralised Information Systems' (1993), paper delivered at *Information and Consultation in Transnational Companies: Exchange of Experiences on Existing Practices*, Gustav-Stresemann-Institut, Bonn, 16-18 May.

'Information and Consultation in Multinational Companies - the Next Steps' (1994), paper delivered at *Nordic Council of Ministers Conference*, Copenhagen, 16-17 February.

'Statutory European Works Councils: the Final Countdown?' (1994), with Mark Hall, in: *Industrial Relations Journal*, Vol. 25, No. 3, September, pp. 177-186.

'Direct Communications in European Multinationals: a Case Study Approach' (1994) Dublin: European Foundation.

RESEARCH SERIES

The Research Series of reports was introduced in March 1992 and supersedes the Department's Research Papers (covering employment and industrial relations issues) and the Training Research and Development series.

Listed below are the current reports in the new series. Copies can be obtained free of charge from Research Strategy and Budgets, Department for Education and Employment, Room W441, Moorfoot, Sheffield S1 4PQ or by contacting our Orderline telephone number 0114 259-3932.

Listing of Research Papers and Training Research and Development reports can be obtained by contacting the above address or telephone number.

RES

No.   Title and author(s)

1. **Measure for Measure**

   A comparative analysis of measures to combat racial discrimination in the member states of the European Community. I Forbes and G Mead, Equal Opportunities Study Group, University of Southampton. 1992.

2. **New Developments in Employee Involvement**

   M Marchington, J Goodman, A Wilkinson and P Ackers, Manchester School of Management, UMIST. 1992.

3. **Entrepreneurship in Cleveland 1979-1989: A Study of the Effects of the Enterprise Culture**

   D J Storey and A Strange, Centre for Small and Medium Sized Enterprises, Warwick Business School, University of Warwick. 1992.

4. **Alcohol Consumption and Sickness Absence: An Analysis of 1984 General Household Survey Data.**

   L M Joeman, Employment Department. 1992.

5. **Payment Systems: A Look at Current Practices.**

   B Casey, J Lakey and M White, Policy Studies Institute. September 1992.

6. **New Inward Investment and the Northern Region Labour Market.**

   F Peck and I Stone, Newcastle Economic Research Unit, University of Northumbria at Newcastle. October 1992.

7. **Final-Offer Arbitration in the UK: Incidence, processes and outcomes.**

   S Milner, Centre for Economic Performance, London School of Economics. January 1993.

8. **Information Requirements in Occupational Decision Making**

   Dr N C Boreham and Dr T A A Arthur, University of Manchester. March 1993.

9. **The Motivation to Train**

   M Crowder and K Pupynin, Minds at Work. April 1993.

10. **TEC Participation in National Development Activity**

   Ernst & Young. May 1993.

11. **Business Growth Training Option 3 Evaluation Project**

J. Neill Marshall, Neil Alderman, Cecilia Wong and Alfred Thwaites, Centre for Urban and Regional Development Studies, University of Newcastle. May 1993.

12. **TECs & employers: Developing effective links. Part 1: a survey.**

Patrick Vaughan, Employment Department. July 1993.

13. **TECs & employers: Developing effective links. Part 2: TEC-employer links in six TEC areas.**

Theresa Crowley-Bainton, Policy Studies Institute. August 1993.

14. **The Abolition of the Dock Labour Scheme.**

N Evans and D MacKay, Pieda plc and M Garratt and P Sutcliffe, MDS Transmodal. September 1993.

15. **New firm formation and small business growth in the United Kingdom: Spatial and temporal variations and determinants**

D Keeble and S Walker, Department of Geography and Small Business Research Centre, University of Cambridge, and M Robson, Department of Economics, University of Newcastle-upon-Tyne. September 1993.

16. **Employment Policies for Disabled People: A review of legislation and services in fifteen countries**

N Lunt and P Thornton, Social Policy Research Unit, University of York. October 1993.

17. **An Evaluation of Supported Employment Initiatives for Disabled People**

A Pozner and J Hammond, OUTSET Consultancy Services (with a contribution by V Tannam, Employment Service). October 1993.

18. **Teleworking in Britain**

Ursula Huws, Analytica. October 1993.

19. **Partnerships for Equality: A review of Employers' Equal Opportunities Groups**

G Whitting, J Moore and P Warren, ECOTEC Research and Consulting Ltd. October 1993.

20. **Factors Influencing Individual Committment to Lifetime Learning**

Malcolm Maguire, Susan Maguire and Alan Felstead, Centre for Labour Market Studies, University of Leicester. December 1993.

21. **Investors in People. A qualitative study of employers.**

A Rix, R Parkinson and R Gaunt, CRG People at Work. January 1994.

22. **The 1992 Survey of Industrial Tribunal Applications**

Nigel Tremlett, Social and Community Planning Research (SCPR) and Nitya Banerji, Employment Department. February 1994.

23. **Thinking and Learning at Work: A report on the development and evaluation of the Thinking Skills At Work modules**

Nigel Blagg, Rachel Lewis and Marj Ballinger, Nigel Blagg Associates. March 1994.

24. **The Early Use of Local Initiative Funds by TECs: Evoking local prosperity**

John Bazalgette, David Armstrong, Jean Hutton and Colin Quine, The Grubb Institute. March 1994.

25. **Regional Advice Units: An examination of models for delivering advice and guidance to TECs and Department of Employment Regional Offices**

Kate Pupynin and Mary Crowder, Minds at Work. April 1994.

26. **The Role of Evaluation in TEC Planning: Final report**

Ian Pearson, WMEB Consultants. April 1994.

27. **The Changing Structure of Occupations and Earnings in Great Britain, 1975-1990. An analysis based on the New Earnings Survey Panel Dataset.**

P Elias and M Gregory, Institute for Employment Research, University of Warwick. May 1994.

28. **Middle Managers: Their Contribution to Employee Involvement**

M Fenton O'Creevy and N Nicholson, Centre for Organisational Research, London Business School. June 1994.

29. **An International Overview of Employment Policies and Practices Towards Older Workers**

J Moore, B Tilson and G Whitting, ECOTEC Research and Consulting Ltd. June 1994.

30. **Training: An exploration of the word and the concept with an analysis of the implications for survey design**

P Campanelli with Roger Thomas, Survey Methods Centre, SCPR, and J Channell with L McAulay and A Renouf, Research & Development Unit for English Studies, University of Birmingham. July 1994.

31. **Individual Commitment to Lifetime Learning: Individuals' Attitudes. Report on the qualitative phase.**

S Taylor and L Spencer, Social and Community Planning Research (SCPR). July 1994.

32. **Individual Commitment to Lifetime Learning: Individuals' Attitudes. Report on the quantitative survey.**

A Park, Social and Community Planning Research (SCPR). July 1994.

33. **Sunday Working. Analysis of an Employer Survey.**

Prof. D Bosworth, Manchester School of Management, UMIST. August 1994.

34. **The Economic Effects of Reductions in Working Hours: the UK Engineering Industry.**

R Richardson and M Rubin, Department of Industrial Relations and Centre for Economic Performance, London School of Economics. September 1994.

35. **Participation and Progress in the Labour Market: Key issues for women.**

L Spencer and S Taylor, Social and Community Planning Research (SCPR). September 1994.

36. **Acting Positively: Positive action under the Race Relations Act 1976.**

C Welsh, J Knox and M Brett, Capita Management Consultancy. October 1994.

37. **The Impact of the Posted Workers' Directive on Company Practice in the United Kingdom.**

M Gold, National Institute of Economic and Social Research. October 1994.

38. **Thematic Evaluation of EHEI.**

C Biggs, R Brighton, P Minnitt, R Pow and W Wicksteed, Segal Quince Wicksteed Ltd. October 1994.

39. **Caring and Employment**

L Corti, H Laurie and S Dex, ESRC Research Centre on Micro-social Change, University of Essex. November 1994.

40. **Individual Commitment to Learning: Employers' Attitudes**

H Metcalf, A Walling and M Fogarty, Policy Studies Institute. November 1994.

41. **Employment and Family Life: A review of research in the UK (1980-1994)**

J Brannen, G Mészáros, P Moss and G Poland, Centre for Research on Family Life and Employment, Thomas Coram Research Unit, Institute of Education, University of London. November 1994.

42. **Individual Commitment to Learning: Individuals' Decision-Making About 'Lifetime Learning'**

A Hand, J Gambles and E Cooper, Quadrangle Consulting Ltd. November 1994.

43. **Household Labour Supply**

S Dex, A Clark and M Taylor, ESRC Research Centre on Micro-social Change, University of Essesx. January 1995.

44. **The Out-of-School Childcare Grant Initiative: An interim evaluation**

I Sanderson and J Percy-Smith, with A Foreman, M Wraight and L Murphy, Policy Research Unit, Leeds Metropolitan University and P Petrie, Thomas Coram Research Unit, University of London. January 1995.

45. **Evaluation of the Open Learning Credits Pilot Programme: Summary report**

T Crowley-Bainton, Policy Studies Institute. January 1995.

46. **TECS and their Non-Employer Stakeholders**

G Haughton, T Hart, I Strange and K Thomas, CUDEM, School of the Environment, Leeds Metropolitan University, and J Peck, SPA, School of Geography, Manchester University. February 1995.

47. **Individual Commitment to Learning: Providers' attitudes**

N Tremlett, A Thomas and S Taylor, Social and Community Planning Research (SCPR). March 1995.

48. **Labour Market Flexibility**

M Beatson, Employment Market Research Unit, Employment Department. April 1995.

49. **The Exercise of Individual Employment Rights in the Member States of the European Community**

C Barnard, J Clark and R Lewis, University of Southampton. April 1995.

50. **Highly Qualified Women**

L Corti, H Laurie and S Dex, ESRC Research Centre on Micro-social Change, University of Essex. April 1995.

51. **Local Development Partnerships and Investments in People**

P Field, J Moore and P Dickinson, The Research Partnership, and J Elgar and P Gray, Oxford Research Ltd. May 1995.

52. **Comparison of Regulations on Part-time and Temporary Employment in Europe**

S Marullo, European Department, Incomes Data Services Ltd. May 1995.

53. **The Cost - Effectiveness of Open and Flexible Learning for TECs**

D Beaton, Ernst & Young. June 1995.

54. **Individual Commitment to Learning: Further Findings from the Individuals' Survey**

N Tremlett, A Park and D Dundon-Smith, Social and Community Planning Research (SCPR). June 1995.

55. **Evaluation of the WRFE Programme**

H Metcalf with C Dawson, Policy Studies Institute. July 1995.

56. **The Evaluation of the National Training Awards**

N Evans, Pieda. August 1995.

57. **Learning Effectiveness of Open and Flexible Learning in Vocational Education: A literature review and annotated bibliography**

A McCollum and J Calder, Institute of Educational Technology, Open University. August 1995.

58. **Learning Effectiveness of Open and Flexible Learning in Vocational Education**

J Calder, A McCollum, A Morgan and M Thorpe, Institute of Educational Technology, Open University. August 1995.

59. **Alcohol in the Workplace: Costs and Responses**

D Hutcheson, M Henderson and J Davies, Centre for Applied Social Psychology, University of Strathclyde. August 1995.

60. **TEC Challenge Evaluation**

T Crowley-Bainton and I Christie with M White, C Dawson and P Taylor, Policy Studies Institute. October 1995.

61. **Measuring 'Broad' Skills: The Prediction of Skill Retention and Transfer Over Time**

A Wolf and R Silver, Institute of Education, University of London. October 1995.

62. **Redundancy in Britain: Findings from the Labour Force Survey**

B Casey, Policy Studies Institute. October 1995.

63. **Cost Effectiveness of Open Learning for Small Firms: A Study of First Experiences of Open Learning**

H Temple, Hilary Temple Associates. October 1995.

64. **TECs and Their Boards**

G Haughton, J Peck, T Hart, I Strange, A Tickell and C Williams, CUDEM, School of the Environment, Leeds Metropolitan University and SPA, School of Geography, Manchester University. October 1995.

65. **A Study of National Vocational Qualification Achievement Through Open and Flexible Learning**

J Calder and W Newton, Institute of Educational Technology, The Open University. October 1995.